STRAIGHTFORWARD
GUIDES

A STRAIGHTFORWARD GUIDE TO FAMILY LAW
Sixth Edition
David Bryan

Dorset County Library	
Askews	2008
346.42015	£8.99

Straightforward Guides
Brighton BN2 4EG

© Straightforward Publishing 2008

All rights reserved. No part of this publication may be reproduced in a retrieval system or transmitted by any means, electronic or mechanical, photocopying or otherwise, without the prior permission of the copyright holder.

British cataloguing in Publication Data. A catalogue record for this book is available from the British Library.

ISBN 1900694 83 2
ISBN 13: 9781900694 83 6

Printed by Biddles Kings Lynn Norfolk

Cover design by Bookworks Islington

Whilst every effort has been made to ensure that the information contained within this book at the time of going to press, the authors and publishers cannot accept liability for any errors and omissions contained within, or for any changes in the law since publication.

CONTENTS

	PP
List of cases	14

Chapter 1
Introduction — 16

Chapter 2
Marriage and Divorce — 21

The definition of marriage	21
The formalities of marriage	21
Nullity, void and voidable Marriages	22
Grounds on which a marriage is void	23
Voidable marriages	25
Judicial separation	26

Chapter 3
Civil Partnerships — 27

Registration of a civil partnership	28
Residency requirements for a civil partnership	29
Special circumstances	30
Housebound people	30
Detained people	31
Family relationships	31
Adoption	31
Parental responsibility	31
Dissolution of a civil partnership	32
Nullity	33

Separation	33
Property and financial arrangements	33

Chapter 4
When a relationship Ends

35

The divorce process	35
Contested petitions	35
The grounds for divorce	36

Chapter 5
Rights of Occupation in the Home

39

Awards of property and financial rewards	39
The Family Law Act 1996	39
The Matrimonial Causes Act 1973 Ancillary to Decree Proceedings	40
Periodic payments secured and unsecured	41
Lump sum	41
Transfer of property	41
Settlement of property order and variation of order	41
Orders for the benefit of children	44
Financial awards-The Domestic proceedings and Magistrates Court Act 1978	44
Financial awards-section 27 of the Matrimonial Causes Act 1973	44
Financial and property awards-section 15 of the Children Act 1989	46
Unmarried partners	46
Establishing a trust	47
An express agreement	48

Quantification of beneficial interests under a trust	49
Proprietary estoppel	50
Occupation of the home	50

Chapter 6
Provision for Children — 52

The Child Support Agency	52
Determining the father	53
Non-disclosure by the resident parent	53
Maintenance requirement	53
Maintenance assessments and special cases	54
Matrimonial Causes Act 1973	56
Matters taken into account when making an order	56
The Children Act 1989 section 15	57

Chapter 7
Domestic Violence — 59

Definition of domestic violence	59
Inherent jurisdiction	60
The Family Law Act 1996 Part 1V	61
Associated persons or relevant child	62
Non-molestation orders	63
Occupation orders	63
The courts powers	64
The balance of harm test	64
Applicant is a former spouse or a cohabitant	64
Former cohabitant with no right to occupy	66
Additional powers	66
The Protection from Harassment Act 1997	67

Enforcement	67
Domestic Violence, Crime and Victims Act 2004	68

Chapter 8
Children and Adults
69

Parents rights and obligations	69
Definition of a parent	69
Biological parents	69
Psychological parents	70
Parenting and the social context	70
The legal parent	71
Parental responsibility	71
Proving parentage	72
Step-parents	73
Adoptive parents	73
Foster parents	74
Parents and reproductive technology	74
Parties separating	74
Meaning of parental responsibility	75
Right to discipline children	76
Right to consent to medical treatment	76
Right to withhold consent for marriage	77

Chapter 9
Adoption
78

The Adoption and Children Act 2002	78
Adoption services	80
Care plans	80
Adoption of children from overseas	80

Who can adopt 81
Suitability 81
Matching parents and children 82
Regulation and review of decisions 82
Court orders 83
Placement order 83
Adoption order 83
Alternatives to adoption orders 84
Adoption by step-parents 84
Discovery and information 84
Human rights and genetic identity 84

Chapter 10 86
Children and the Human Rights Act

United Nations Convention on the Rights of 86
The Child
Definition of a child 86
The European Convention on Human Rights 89
Freestanding human rights applications in family cases 89
A local authority failure to protect children 90
Procedural rights 90
Proportionality of response 91

Chapter 11 93
Protection of Children and the resolution of Disputes

Residence order 93
Contact order 93
Prohibited steps order 94
Specific issues order 94

Different types of proceedings	94
Types of applicant	95
Those entitled to apply for a residence or contact order	95
Protection of children-local authorities	96
Types of order available	96
Care orders	96
Supervision orders	97
Emergency protection orders	97
The child assessment order	97
Grounds on which a court will grant an order	99
Parental contact	100
Wardship	100
The Children and Young Person's Bill	100

Chapter 12   104
Rights of Adolescents

The foetus and rights	104
Rights of infants and young children	105
The rights of the adolescent	106

Chapter 13   108
Making a Will

Making a will	109
Divorced persons	111
Separated persons	112
Cohabitation	112
The decision to make a will	112
Ownership of property	113
Children	113

Marriage or remarriage	113
Employment	114
Illness	114
Divorced and separation	114
Increase in personal wealth	114
The provisions of a will	115
Money you have saved	115
Property	115
Land	116
Insurance policies	116
Shares	116
Trusts	116
Personal effects	117
The funeral	117
Use of body after death	118
Making a recital	118
Making provisions in a will	118
Mental illness	119
Bankruptcy	119
Leaving money to charities	120
Preparing a will	121
Choice of an executor	122
Probate	130
Applying for probate	131

Index

List of cases

Pp

R v Inhabitants of Darlington (1972)	16
Gammas v Elikins (1950)	16
Langdon v Horton (1951)	16
Ross v Collins (1964)	17
Fitzpatrick v Sterling Housing Association	18
Ghaidon v Mendoza (2004)	18
Hyde v Hyde (1866)	21
De Reneville v de Reneville (1948)	13
Pugh v Pugh (1951)	24
Gereis v Yacoub (1977)	25
Livingstone-Stallard v Livingstone Stallard (H.C 1974).	37
Le Brocq v. Le Brocq (1964)	37
Suter v. Suter and Jones (C.A. 1986)	42
Leadbeater v Leadbeater (1985)	42
Petit v. Petit (1969)	47
Gissing V.Gissing (1979)	47
(Passee v. Passee (C.A. 1988).	50
Coombes v. Smith (H.C. 1987)	50
Tanner v. Tanner (C.A. 1975)	51
Vaughn v Vaughn (1973)	59
Horner v. Horner (1983)	60
Patel v. Patel (1988)	60
Ashbury v. Millington (1986)	61
Re KD (a minor) (Ward: termination of access) (1988)	69
Re O; Re J (children) (Blood Tests: Constraint) (2000)	73
Re R (a child) (IVF Paternity of Child) (2005),	75
Re H (minors) (Wardship: Cultural background) (1987)	76
Frette v France (2003)	79

C (Adoption: Religious Observance (2002) 82
Paton v British Pregnancy Advisory Service, (1978) 104
Re J and K (Abduction: Objections of Child) (2005) 105
Gillick v West Norfolk and Wisbech Health Authority
(1986) 106

Chapter 1

Introduction

The area of family law is a very complex area, multi-faceted, including every aspect of law and legal intervention into the lives, both private and domestic, of those who are related by blood or by association.

Looking at historical definitions of the meaning of 'family' this encompassed a wide group of people who shared the same household. Obviously, earlier interpretations could, in the light of the 21st century, be seen as outdated and oppressive. For example, in R v Inhabitants of Darlington (1792) Lord Kenyon CJ stated that: 'in common parlance the family consists of those who live under the same roof with the pater familias: those who form…his fireside'. Servants were also included in this definition, often living with the same family for the whole of their lives.

Over the years the law has evolved, as law tends to do. By the twentieth century, legal intervention in family life developed along with definitions of family. Rent Act legislation helped to frame definitions of what was and was not family. In Langdon v Horton (1951) the Court of Appeal refused Rent Act protection to two elderly women who had shared the same house with their cousin for 30 years. The cousin held the house on a statutory tenancy prior to her death. The Court of Appeal held that they had lived together for the sake of convenience and not because they were part of the same family, even though they were cousins.

The following case demonstrates just how much the law has changed. In Gammans v Ekins (1950) the Court of Appeal rejected the claim of a male cohabitant to remain in the family home on the death of his partner. Asquith LJ took the view that either the relationship was platonic and the couple were not members of each other's family or it was not. If the relationship was platonic Asquith LJ believed that to recognize the cohabitants as members of the same family would also require the court to accord the same status to two 'old cronies' of the same sex innocently sharing the same flat. If the relationship were not platonic, Asquith LJ thought it:

'anomalous that a person could acquire a Rent Act protected status by living or have lived in sin, even if the relationship had not been a mere casual encounter but protracted in time and conclusive in character'.

He concluded by saying that to accept a same-sex couple, masquerading as husband and wife, as members of the same family was an abuse of the English language. In Ross v Collins, 1964, a woman claimed the right to succeed to a statutory tenancy on the death of her partner. She had lived with the deceased for a substantial amount of time and was significantly younger than him, 40 years younger, and had looked after him as an elderly relative. Russell LJ ruled that this platonic relationship was not within the definition of family because there was no kinship between the couple. He stated:

'two strangers cannot ever establish artificially a family nexus by acting as brothers or as sisters, even if they refer to each other as thus…….Nor can an adult man and woman who establish a platonic relationship establish a family nexus by acting as a devoted brother and sister or father and daughter would act'.

However, by 1980, the courts had begun to recognize that those living in a stable heterosexual cohabiting relationship could be classified as each other's family. In Watson v Lucas (1980) it was held that a married man, who had left his wife and had lived with the deceased woman in a stable and long-term relationship, was a member of the family for Rent Act purposes.

The above case marked the departure from traditional ways of thinking. Another case which was a landmark ruling, Fitzpatrick v Sterling Housing Association (2000), accepted that homosexuals could be members of each others families. Lord Slynn, in his judgment, viewed the essential hallmarks of a family relationship as a degree of mutual interdependence, the sharing of lives, the caring and love for each other, and the commitment and support for each other.

In Ghaidan v Mendoza (2004) the House of Lords further defined family and held that the term 'husband and wife' in Rent Act legislation could be read to mean 'as if they were husband and wife'. It, therefore, included a same-sex partner who had lived with the deceased in a spouse-like manner.

The concept of family and spouse has been further extended since these landmark decisions. In accordance with the Gender Recognition Act 2004, transgendered persons, who have obtained a gender recognition certificate, may marry a member of the opposite sex to that of their newly acquired gender. Prior to the Act this was not the case. The Civil Partnership Act 2004 has also given a quasi-spousal and familial status to same sex couples who register their partnerships.

The law has moved on significantly, as can be seen. However, there are categories of excluded relationships that need further discussion.

Excluded relationships

There are two categories of relationship, which although functionally familial, have only been granted limited legal rights. The first category consists of cohabiting heterosexual couples and also same-sex cohabitants who have not registered a civil partnership. The Government has asked the Law Commission to undertake a review of the above category. The second category consists of those who live together in the same household as members of the same family but have never engaged in sexual relationships with each other. This is because they are either closely related or because they are close friends who have assumed a personal responsibility for each other but a sexual relationship is considered inappropriate.

The increasing emphasis in family law today centers on the needs, rights and overall welfare of children from conception to adulthood. Parenthood is no longer primarily based on marital status and its definition has evolved to cover new forms of biological and social parent/child relationships. More complex means of assisted reproduction present new challenges to legal concepts of parenthood. At the time of writing, there is a new Human Fertilisation and Embryology Bill working its way through the political process. There are a number of clauses within the Bill which will always be contentious, a reduction in the maximum time limit (currently 24 weeks) after which an abortion is not possible and also the rights of women to no longer have to take into account the role of a father figure. This Bill has, not unnaturally, caused clashes over questions of discrimination, parenthood and the very nature of family life.

In addition, at the time of writing, the Children's and Young Person's Bill is making its way through the political process. The purpose of the Bill is to reform the statutory framework for the care system by implementing the proposals in the June 2007 White paper Care Matters: Time for Change. The Bill forms part of the government's drive to improve the quality of services and support for looked after children. It includes provision in relation to private fostering, child death notification to Local Safeguarding Children's Boards and the Secretary of State's powers to conduct research and applications for the discharge of emergency protection orders. This Bill is summarized in chapter 11, Protection of Children

Another area which taxes all concerned is the financial implications of relationship breakdown. The emphasis is on the importance of recognizing equality between male and female roles and the establishment of rights in the family home.

The above outlines some of the complexities of family law and also illustrates that we have moved from a basic, paternalistic, mode of recognition of family to a more enlightened view, which encompasses much wider concepts such as same-sex relationships. The law dealing with family and family related matters is ever changing and this book brings the reader up to date with legal changes in the new millennium, including the Human Rights Act and issues following on from the passage of this particular legislation in the United Kingdom. In addition, adoption is covered in depth and the Adoption and Children Act 2002 is covered.

It is hoped that by reading this book a valuable insight will be gained into this particular area of law. It must be stressed that this is very much an introduction, and is designed to be read and understood by all sections of the community. It will be equally valuable to the layperson as well as the student.

Chapter 2

Marriage and Divorce

The definition of marriage

Traditionally, the definition of marriage has been rather simple, which is 'marriage is the voluntary union for life of one man and one woman to the exclusion of all others'. (Hyde v Hyde 1866).

Obviously, in the light of the law today, this is outdated and has been superseded. The Gender Recognition Act 2004 (GRA) highlights the fact that marriage is no longer between those who were born respectively male and female. In addition, the ready availability and ease of divorce renders Hyde v Hyde unsatisfactory as a definition. In the following chapter we will explore marriage as a legal concept.

For a marriage to be valid, the marriage must have been entered into voluntarily. The parties must intend it to be for life. It must be a monogamous relationship. Both parties must be over 16 and if under 18 must have the consent of those who have parental responsibility. The Marriage Act 1949, as amended by the Marriage (Prohibited Degrees of Relationship) Act 1986 and the GRA 2004 lists those who may not marry.

In order to marry, a person must be capable of understanding the marriage contract. Mental incapacity can render a contract null and void.

The formalities of marriage

The Marriage Act 1949 requires:

- for a Church of England wedding – the publication of banns, a license, or a certificate of a superintendent registrar or naval officer:
- for other marriages – a certificate of a superintendent registrar.

Marriages can be solemnized in:
- a church or chapel of the Church of England
- a registered non-conformist church or other building
- premises approved by the local authority
- any place if a special license is obtained.

Jews and Quakers may marry according to their own customs with a certificate of a superintendent registrar.

Now that the Gender Recognition Act 2004 is in force, transsexuals will be able to marry according to their 'acquired gender'. Section 1 of the GRA permits transgendered persons to apply for a gender recognition certificate from the Gender Recognition Panel which was set up to determine the gender identity of both pre-operative and post-operative transgendered persons over the age of 18. The certificate allows them to acquire a new gender from that of their birth. They need not have undergone gender realignment surgery if it is inappropriate to do so.

Nullity, void and voidable marriages.

A court can grant a decree of nullity of marriage. Such a decree declares the marriage to be null and void. This is quite different from a termination of marriage.

A void marriage is a marriage that was never a marriage at all. A voidable marriage is a valid marriage until annulled by decree. As a result the parties to such a marriage must obtain a decree before they are entitled to behave as single people.

There are four grounds for nullity, under section 11 of the Matrimonial Causes Act 1973 (MCA). They are:
(a) that it was never a valid marriage under the Marriage Acts;
(b) that at the time of the marriage either party was already lawfully married;
(c) that the parties are not respectively male and female
(d) in the case of a polygamous marriage entered into outside England and Wales, that either party was at the time of the marriage domiciled in England and Wales.

The most common ground used is where one of the parties was already married.

Void marriages

In de Reneville v de Reneville (1948) a void marriage was described as one which never came into existence. No matter how long the parties had lived together, they can never acquire the status of man and wife.

Grounds on which a marriage is void

The Matrimonial Causes Act 1973, s11 provides the grounds for a void marriage:

S 11(a) that it fails to meet the provisions of the Marriage Acts in that
(i) the parties are within the prohibited degrees of relationship.

No one may marry a person to whom they are related by blood or marriage within the prohibited degrees laid down in the Acts. The Marriage Act 1949 as amended by the Marriage (Prohibited Degrees of Relationship) Act 1986 and the GRA 2004 lists those relatives who may not marry. This includes both blood relationships and relationships of affinity:

- father/daughter
- mother/son
- niece/uncle
- nephew/ aunt
- brother/sister
- grandparent/grandchild
- half-siblings
- adopted child/adoptive parent

A person may marry his or her adopted sibling, his or her step-child if both parties are over 21 years of age and if the child, prior to the age of 18, has never been a child of the family in relation to him or her. Marriage between a daughter-in-law or son-in-law with a parent in law is permitted if both parties are over the age of 21 and their former spouses are both dead.

(ii) either party is under the age of 16. In Pugh v Pugh (1951) Pearce J stated:

'According to modern thought, it is socially and morally wrong that persons of an age at which we now believe them to be immature and provide for their education should have the stresses, responsibilities and sexual freedom of marriage and the physical strain of childbirth. Child marriages, by common consent, are believed to be bad for the participants and bad for the institution of marriage. Acts making carnal knowledge of young girls an offence are an indication of modern views on this subject. The remedy that Parliament has resolved for this mischief and defect is to make marriages void where either of the parties is under 16 years of age'.

A person domiciled in England cannot evade the law by marrying in a country where the law is different.

(iii) the parties have intermarried in disregard of certain requirements as to the formation of marriage.

One case that highlights this is Gereis v Yacoub (1977). The parties went through a marriage ceremony or a purported marriage ceremony at a Coptic Orthodox Church knowing that it was not licensed to carry out marriages under the Marriage act 1949. Although this fact would not have made the marriage void they also knew that the priest was not licensed to conduct the ceremony and that notice of marriage had not been given to the superintendent registrar. The priest had advised the coupe that a civil ceremony should take place but they did not do this so the marriage was void.

Section 11 (b) that at the time of the marriage either party was already married or in a civil partnership. Such a marriage is void.

Section 11(c) that the parties are not respectively male and female. Same sex-marriages are not permitted under English law.

Section 11(d) in the case of a polygamous marriage entered into outside England and Wales, that either party was, at the time, domiciled in England and Wales. Polygamous marriages celebrated abroad have become a common occurrence in England with immigrants returning to their country of origin where polygamous marriages are legal, and marry. However, if either party to the marriage is domiciled in England the marriage will be void.

Voidable marriages

Section 12 of the Matrimonial Causes Act details six grounds that are available for declaring a marriage voidable. They are:
(a) non-consummation of marriage due to the incapacity of either party
(b) non-consummation of marriage due to the willful refusal of the respondent
(c) lack of valid consent to the marriage by either party

(d) that either party was suffering from mental disorder
(e) that the respondent was suffering from VD in a communicable form at the time of the marriage
(f) that the respondent was pregnant by someone other than the petitioner at the time of marriage.

The grounds most petitioners use for annulment of a voidable marriage are those relating to non-consummation.

Judicial Separation

Although most whose marriage has broken down will get divorced, there are some who, for various reasons will not wish to terminate the marriage, for example for religious reasons. A judicial separation suits such circumstances and although it does not terminate the marriage it will effectively relieve the petitioner of the responsibility of cohabiting with the other party.

Other people may go for judicial separation because they wish to obtain one of the financial orders that a court has the power to make once a separation is granted. The grounds for judicial separation mirror the five facts for divorce. They fall within section 17(1) of the Matrimonial Causes Act.

Chapter 3

Civil Partnerships

A Civil partnership is a new legal relationship, which can be registered by two people of the same sex. Same-sex couples, within a civil partnership can obtain legal recognition for their relationship and can obtain the same benefits generally as married couples.

The Civil Partnership Act 2004 came into force on 5th December 2005. The first civil partnerships registered in England and Wales took place on 21st December 2005. Civil partners will be treated the same as married couples in many areas, including:

- Tax, including inheritance tax
- Employment benefits
- Most state and occupational pension benefits
- Income related benefits, tax credits and child support
- Maintenance for partner and children
- Ability to apply for parental responsibility for a civil partners child
- Inheritance of a tenancy agreement
- Recognition under intestacy rules
- Access to fatal accidents compensation
- Protection from domestic violence
- Recognition for immigration and nationality purposes

The registration of a civil partnership

Two people may register a civil partnership provided they are of the same sex, not already in a civil partnership or legally married, not closely related and both over 16 although consent of a parent or guardian must be obtained if either of them are under 18.

Registering a civil partnership is a secular procedure and is carried out by the registration service, which is responsible for the registration of births, deaths and marriages. A civil partnership registration is carried out under what is termed a standard procedure, which can be varied to take into account housebound people or people who are ill and are not expected to recover.

The standard procedure for registering a civil partnership

A couple wishing to register a civil partnership just have to decide the date they want to register and where they want the registration to take place. The formal process for registering consists of two main stages-the giving of a notice of intention to register and then the registration of the civil partnership itself.

The first stage, the giving of notice is a legal requirement and both partners have to do this at a register office in the area of a local authority where they live, even if they intend to register elsewhere. The notice contains the names, age, marital or civil partnership status, address, occupation, nationality and intended venue for the civil partnership. It is a criminal offence to give false information. If one of the partners is a non-EAA citizen and subject to immigration controls (see later) there are additional requirements to be fulfilled. Once the notice has been given it is displayed at the relevant register office for 15 days. This provided an opportunity for objections to be made. The civil partnership cannot be registered until after 15 clear days have elapsed from the date of the second person gives notice.

Each partner needs to give notice in the area that they have lived for at least seven days. If the couple live in different areas then each will post a notice in their own relevant area. When giving notice they will be asked where they wish the civil partnership to take place.

Residency requirements for a civil partnerships

A couple can register a civil partnership in England and Wales as long as they have both lived in a registration district in England and Wales for at least seven days immediately before giving notice. If one person lives in Scotland and the other lives in England or Wales, the person living in Scotland may give notice there. Officers, sailors or marines on board a Royal Navy ship at sea can give notice to the captain or other commanding officer, providing they are going to register with someone who is resident in England and Wales. Service personnel based outside England and Wales have to fulfil the above residence requirements.

Documentary evidence of name, age and nationality will need to be shown. Passports and birth certificates are the main documents required. Proof of address will be required. If either partner has been married or in a civil partnership before evidence of divorce or dissolution will be required. If either partner is subject to immigration control a document showing entry clearance granted to form a civil partnership will need to be shown, along with a home office certificate of approval and indefinite leave to remain in the UK.

Civil partnership registration

A civil partnership registration can take place in any register office in England and Wales or at any venue that has been approved to hold a civil partnership. Approved premises include stately homes and other prestigious buildings including hotels and restaurants. From 5th December 2005, any venue that has approval for civil marriage will automatically be approved for civil partnerships. A civil partnership cannot be registered at a religious premises. A civil partnership can only be registered between the hours of 8am to 6pm unless one person is seriously ill and is not expected to recover.

A civil partnership is legally registered once the couple have signed the legal document, known as a civil partnership schedule, in the presence of a registrar and two witnesses. On the day, two witnesses will be required. If they wish to do so, the couple will be able to speak to each other the words contained in the schedule:

' I declare that I know of no legal reason why we may not register as each other's civil partner. I understand that on signing this document we will be forming a civil partnership with each other'

No religious service may take place, as the process of forming a civil partnership is entirely secular. A ceremony can be arranged to accompany the actual registration. This ceremony can take place at any venue as long as it is approved.

Special circumstances

Variations to the standard procedure can be made in certain circumstances. If a partner is seriously ill and is not expected to recover then a civil partnership can be registered at any time. The 15-day waiting period will not apply. A certificate will need to be provided from a doctor stating that a person is not expected to recover and cannot be moved to a place where civil partnerships take place and that they understand the nature and purpose of signing the Registrar Generals licence.

Housebound people

If one partner is housebound there are special procedures to allow them to register a civil partnership at home. A statement has to be signed, made by a doctor, confirming that this is the case and that the condition is likely to continue for the next three months. The statement must have been made no more than 14 days before notice being given and must be made on a standard form provided by the register office. The normal 15-day period will apply between giving notice and the civil partnership registration.

Detained people

There are special procedures to allow a couple to register a civil partnership at a place where one of them is detained in a hospital or prison. The couple has to provide a statement, made by the prison governor or responsible person confirming that the place where a person is detained can be named in the notice of proposed civil partnership as the place where the registration is to take place. This statement must have been made no more than 21 days prior to notice being given. The normal 15 day waiting period applies.

Family relationships

The law now recognises the role of both civil partners in respect of a child living in their household.

Adoption

Under the Adoption and Children Act 2002, which came into force on 30th December 2005, civil partners may apply jointly to adopt a child.

Parental responsibility

Under the Adoption and Children Act 2002, a person will also be able to acquire parental responsibility for the child of their civil partner. They can do this with the agreement of their civil partner.

If the child's other parent also has parental responsibility, both parents must agree. Parental responsibility can also be acquired on application to the court. Civil partners will have a duty to provide maintenance for each other and any children of the civil partnership.

Dissolution of a civil partnership

A civil partnership ends only on the death of one of the civil partners, or on the dissolution of the partnership or a nullity order or a presumption of death order by the court.

The usual route is for one of the partners to seek a dissolution order to terminate the civil partnership. Other options are available. If one party, for example, did not validly consent as a result of duress, mistake or unsoundness of mind, then a nullity order may be sought from the court. Or if both civil partners do not wish to terminate the partnership one of them may ask the court for a separation order.

The dissolution process

Whoever decides to end the civil partnership should seek legal advice. The case will usually be dealt with by a civil partnership proceedings county court, although complex cases will be referred to the high court.

To end a civil partnership the applicant (petitioner) must prove to the court that the civil partnership has irretrievably broken down. Proof of an irretrievable breakdown is based on the following:

- Unreasonable behaviour by one or other civil partner
- Separation for two years with the consent of the other civil partner
- Separation for five years without the consent of the other civil partner
- If the other civil partner has deserted the applicant for a period of two years or more.

Nullity
In exceptional circumstances one party to a civil partnership may decide to seek a court order (a 'Nullity' order) to annul the civil partnership.

Separation
The grounds on which a separation order may be sought are exactly the same as those for a dissolution order. The end result is different, as a person whose civil partnership has been dissolved is free to marry or form a new partnership whereas a person who has separated remains a civil partner.

Property and financial arrangements
If a civil partnership is ending or if the couple are separating, they will need to decide what happens to any property belonging to them. If they agree on a division they can ask the court to approve the agreement. If they cannot agree they can ask the court to decide. The court has power to make a range of orders in relation to property and other assets including income:

- The court can make an order that one civil partner pay maintenance to the other either for the benefit of the civil partner or for the benefit of any children of the relationship. These orders are known as financial provision orders.
- The court can make an order which will adjust the property rights of the civil partners as regards to property and other assets which they own, either together or separately. This may, for example, mean ordering the transfer and ownership of property from one civil partner to another for that persons benefit or the benefit of any children (known as property adjustment orders)
- The court can make an order in relation to the future pension entitlement of one of the civil partners in favour of the other.

This order can relate to occupational pensions, personal pensions and other annuities (known as pension sharing orders)

Financial provision orders for maintenance can be made before a civil partnership has been ended or as separation order granted by the court. Property adjustment and pension sharing orders only take legal effect once dissolution, separation or nullity order has been made by the court.

Even if the couple have been able to agree on maintenance and other property issues they should seek professional advice on such issues. In most cases the solicitor dealing with the end of the civil partnership will be able to provide appropriate advice.

Chapter 4

When a Relationship Ends

Divorce is the legal process which married couples must go through if they wish to end their marriage formally and revert to a single status.

The United Kingdom has often been referred to as the divorce capital of the world. Whilst that may be an exaggerated claim, in this country 40% of marriages end in divorce, most of them in the age group 25-29. There are many factors attributed to this high rate, not least the increased life span of people and greater economic independence of women. Whatever the explanation, the consequences are severe for society. Children are quite often victims but there are other effects such as increased welfare benefits and stress and depression with the consequent implications for the health system.

The divorce process

The actual procedure for getting divorced is relatively simple. It is an administrative process, rather than a judicial process and is known as the 'special procedure'. Those involved do not normally have to appear in court. One of the spouses, referred to as the petitioner will fill in a set of forms and sign an affidavit confirming the truth of the petition. These will be inspected by a district judge who, if satisfied that all is in order will issue a certificate and a divorce decree will be granted.

Contested petitions

Very few petitions are contested, less than 3%, but if one is contested then there will be a full hearing in front of a judge. A decree of divorce will only be refused when the respondent is able to prove that the petitioners factual statement is incorrect and that the marriage remains viable.

The divorce decree is divided into two parts-the decree nisi, which is the first part and which is announced in open court, usually without the attendance of the parties. The second part, the decree absolute is granted after a period of six weeks has elapsed. Only when the decree absolute is granted can the parties remarry.

Before the court grants the decree, it must be satisfied that arrangements have been made for the welfare of the children under the Matrimonial Causes Act 1973 s 41. If it is not satisfied it will delay the decree absolute.

Divorce-The Ground For Divorce

The Matrimonial Causes Act 1973 governs all matters relating to divorce.

Section 1(1) of the Act states that there is one ground for divorce, that is that the person making an application for a divorce, known as the petitioner, must establish that the marriage has irretrievably broken down. There are two further requirements. First the petitioner must have been married for at least one year and secondly where it is self-evident that the marriage has broken down the petitioner must prove five facts laid down in s 1(2) of the Act:

(a) that the respondent has committed adultery and the petitioner finds it intolerable to live with him/ her.
Section 2 (1) of the Matrimonial Causes Act 1973 states that there can be no decree if the parties have lived with each other for more than six months after the discovery of the alleged adultery.

(b) that the respondent has behaved in such a way that the petitioner cannot reasonably be expected to live with him.

When deciding on whether this fact is proved, the court will take into account the characters and personalities of individuals and will attempt objectively to arrive at an interpretation of reasonableness. One significant case was Livingstone-Stallard v Livingstone Stallard (H.C 1974). According to the judge in that case, Dunn j. the question that must be answered is: "Would any right thinking person come to the conclusion that this husband has behaved in such a way that this wife cannot be reasonably expected to live with him, taking into account the whole of the circumstances and the characters and personalities of the parties".

(c) that the respondent has deserted the petitioner for a period of at least two years immediately preceding the presentation of the petition.
A very small percentage of divorce petitions rely on desertion. There are four conditions that must be fulfilled before a spouse will be found to be in desertion:

(a) the parties must be physically living apart
(b) the deserting spouse must have the requisite intention
(c) the separation must not have taken place as a result of an agreement between the parties
(d) the deserting spouse must have had good cause for leaving.
(e) that the parties have lived apart for a continuous period of at least two years immediately preceding the presentation of the petition and the respondent consents to a decree being granted

This fact has two aspects: the period of living apart and the respondents consent. "Living apart" can mean living under the same roof and not living as man and wife, in addition to one party leaving the other. One key case here was Le Brocq v. Le Brocq (1964) where a wife excluded her husband from her bedroom by fixing a bolt on the door. The two parties communicated only when necessary. However she cooked his meals and he paid her weekly housekeeping. It was found that although there was a separation of bedrooms there still existed one household.

d) that the parties have lived apart for a period of at least five years immediately preceding the presentation of the petition.
There are several key differences between this section. the first is length of time the parties have to have been apart and the fact that the petitioner does not need the other parties consent. However, under section five of the Matrimonial Homes Act the respondent can file a defence that the resulting divorce would mean grave financial or other hardship to him/her and that it would be wrong on these grounds to resolve the marriage. If the court finds that the petitioner can establish another fact for divorce then this undermines the above defence. The Court will not grant a divorce unless one of these five facts has been proved. The court can refuse to grant a decree if it is satisfied that the marriage has not broken down. No petition for divorce can be filed unless the parties have been married for one year.

Chapter 5

Rights of Occupation in the Home

Awards of property and financial awards.

The Family Law Act 1996

When homes are vested in one person, complications can arise during or after a divorce. At common law, even though the home (estate) may be vested in the husband, the wife has the right to occupy it. However, this right could be completely undermined by sale of the estate to a third party.

Section 30 of the FLA applies where one spouse (owner) has the right to occupy property that is or was the matrimonial home and the other has not, the other is given 'matrimonial home rights' in that property. There is a right not to be evicted from it without leave of the court and the right to resume occupation if the non-owner is not in occupation (there has been some attempt to evict, for example).

The spouse will only receive benefit of the Act if she needs it. A spouse who already has rights of occupation is not entitled to the statutory rights. Section 30 (9) of the FLA specifically provides that a spouse who only has an equitable interest in the home, and not a legal estate, is to be treated as not being entitled to occupy the house by virtue of that interest. This is of some significance when seeking occupation orders.

The rights exist until termination of the marriage. The rights can also be restricted or terminated by an earlier court order under the FLA s 33 (5).

Creation of rights of occupation between spouses is not the only objective achieved by the FLA. The non-owning spouse must register matrimonial home rights as either a land charge, Class F (for unregistered land), or a notice, for unregistered land. If this is done, then any subsequent purchaser for value will take subject to the statutory rights of occupation. It should be noted, however, that he then has the same rights to apply to the courts for termination or restriction of the matrimonial home rights and his own circumstances, as well as the spouse's, can be taken into account.

The Matrimonial Causes Act 1973 Ancillary to Decree proceedings
The above are orders for the benefit of spouses. By sections 23 and 24 of the Matrimonial Causes Act 1973 the court can grant one or more of the following orders for the benefit of a spouse against another:

(a) periodical payments order
(b) a secured periodical payments order
(c) an order for lump sum or sums
(d) a transfer of property order
(e) a settlement of property order
(f) a variation of settlement order
(g) an order extinguishing an interest in a settlement.

None of these orders can be made until a decree of divorce, nullity or judicial separation has been granted. Therefore, if the divorce proceedings fail, no order for a spouse can be made under the MCA, ss 23 and 24. All of these orders can be made on the grant of a decree or after. However, a spouse is barred from an order if he or she has remarried prior to the application.

Now that the Family Law Act has come fully into force, there will be a change in that these orders will have to be made or agreed before a decree of divorce or separation can be granted. There is also a pilot scheme in operation in a number of courts with practice directions aimed at reducing delay and costs, encouraging settlements and giving courts greater control over proceedings.

Periodic payments secured and unsecured

This is an order (MCA s23) where one spouse should pay another a periodic sum of money. If it is secured this means that it is charged upon a property owned by the spouse. Secured payments can continue beyond the death of a spouse, unsecured payments do not. The court has the power to vary or terminate an order. Apart from automatic termination, the court itself has the power to control the duration of both forms of periodical payment. It can order the payments to be made for only a specific length of time and, in addition, can direct that at the end of the specified period the recipient should not be entitled to ask for an extension of the period.

Lump sum

This is an order where one spouse pays another a fixed sum or sums of money. If the lump sum is to be paid in installments then it can be secured on a property.

Transfer of property

This is an order that one spouse transfers to the other property to which the former is entitled. Property can cover anything from houses and flats, jewelry, vehicles, furniture and so on. The M.C.A does not define property. Even if the matrimonial home is mortgaged, it can be the subject of a transfer order, and likewise if it is rented (except for a statutory tenancy under the Rent Act).

Settlement of property order and variation of settlement order

The former is an order that one spouse settle property to which he/she is entitled for the benefit of another. Property is widely interpreted. The variation of a settlement order is an order that any ante- or post-nuptial settlement made on the spouse should be varied for their benefit.

By section 25(1) of the M.C.A. it is provided that, when deciding whether and how to exercise its powers, the court must consider all the circumstances of the case, but give first consideration to the welfare of any minor children of the family. In Suter v. Suter and Jones (C.A. 1986) it was held that giving first consideration to the welfare of the children in financial proceedings did not mean that the welfare of the children overrode all other considerations.

The Child Support Act affects the above, however, where child maintenance is calculated using rigid formula under the jurisdiction of the Child Support Agency, discussed further in chapter 5.

Section 25(2) of the Matrimonial Causes Act directs the court to have regard to the following factors when exercising their powers to make financial provision for a spouse:

a) Income, earning capacity, property and other financial resources. The courts must have regard to the income and capital of both parties, including any that they are likely to have in the foreseeable future. Income includes both earned and unearned income. Capital includes all land, investments, cash and personal possessions. A party's earning capacity is also a resource, including that he is likely to have in the foreseeable future.

One such case in this respect is Leadbeater v Leadbeater (1985) where the wife, aged 47, had been a secretary before marriage but the court thought it unreasonable for her to learn new skills. However, she could have worked longer at her job as a receptionist and her notional earnings were set at £2550, as opposed to her actual income of £1,700.

b) Financial needs, obligations and responsibilities. Again, the court must have regard to all such matters, including those that the parties are likely to have in the foreseeable future. This includes living expenses. Any liabilities of a capital nature are taken into account, such as outstanding mortgage.

(c) Standards of living (enjoyed by family prior to breakdown). In some cases the court will exercise its powers so that the marriage breakdown will have the least possible effect on the standard of living of the parties.

(d) Age of parties and duration of marriage. The age of the parties must be taken into account by the court and can be relevant for a number of reasons. For example, the age of a person may affect promotion prospects or, indeed, whether a job can be found after all.

The duration of the marriage must also be taken into account by the court. There is no definition of what is long or short, but a short marriage is usually taken to mean one of only a few years. Generally, the parties to a short marriage will have less claim on each other than those who have been married for a longer time. However, even a marriage of a shorter duration can produce children, and short marriages between older couples can mean a change in their positions, for example the loss of pension rights previously accrued.

(e) Disabilities. The court must take into account any physical or mental disability of either of the parties to the marriage.

f) Contributions to the welfare of the family. It is specifically provided that this includes any contribution made by looking after the home or caring for the family. Thus the wife, who gives up her job and contributes nothing to the family in hard cash, but is the home-maker and child rearer, has the value of such activities recognised.

g) Conduct. This is a vague principle and relates to gross misconduct, one party against another.

h) The value of any lost benefit. In divorce and nullity cases, the court must take into account the value of any benefit the parties lose the chance of acquiring. This could be, for example, pension rights, which parties might lose on a decree being granted. In Brooks v Brooks, for example, the court compensated the wife by leaving the pension with the husband but giving her other assets. Section 166 of the Pensions Act 1995 enables the court to 'earmark' pensions, that is, to order pension fund managers to pay specific sums to the spouse even where the pension payments are deferred.

In addition to the factors listed above, there are additional considerations for the courts. By section 25A(1) of the M.C.A. the court is placed under a duty to consider whether it is appropriate to make orders that will terminate the parties financial obligations to each other as soon after the decree as it thinks reasonable. Section 25A(2) creates another obligation on the court. If it has decided that an order for periodical payments must be made (this not ordering a clean break) then it must consider whether to order that the payments must cease after a specified period, a period designed to permit an adjustment to financial independence without undue hardship. T

The court has no duty to order a clean break, immediate or delayed; it gives a duty to consider only whether it should order a clean break in every case where it was asked to exercise its financial powers on divorce (or nullity).

Orders for the benefit of children

Children of the family can have the same types of orders made in their favour, against either parties of the marriage, as can the parties themselves. Chapter 5 discusses this in further depth.

Financial awards - The Domestic Proceedings and Magistrates Court Act 1978

It may be the case that one party may want an order against another but cannot or does not wish to issue decree proceedings. The D.P.M.C.A. is one of several statutes that gives the courts power to order financial relief without the necessity of first obtaining an order relating to the status of the marriage itself. Three different situations are covered by the Act.

Sections 1 and 2 of the D.P.M.C.A.

Although the applicant is not seeking any type of decree, he still has to establish one of the following grounds set out in section 2:
(a) that the respondent has failed to provide reasonable maintenance for the applicant;
(b) that the respondent has failed to provide or make proper contribution towards the reasonable maintenance of a child of the family;
(c) that the respondent has behaved in such a way that the applicant cannot reasonably be expected to live with him;
(d) that the respondent has deserted the applicant.

There is no definition of the term "reasonable maintenance" in the Act. The court has to take into account the parties respective positions in making their determination. Once the applicant has proved one of the grounds the court has the power to do the following:

(a) make an order that the respondent should pay periodical payments to the applicant and/or a child of the family;
(b) that the respondent should pay a lump sum to the applicant and/or a child of the family, such lump sum not to exceed £1,000.

Orders for periodical payments cease on the death of the payer. Orders for periodical payments to a spouse cease on remarriage of the spouse. The rules for cessation of payments to children are the same as under the Matrimonial Causes Act. Further, orders for periodical payments that are payable to a spouse, either for herself or a child, cease if the parties continue to cohabit or resume cohabitation after the making of the order for a period or periods exceeding six months. Once a ground is proved, a court has to decide whether to make any order at all. Welfare of children is the usual first consideration.

Financial awards - section 27 of the Matrimonial Causes Act 1973

The courts can grant periodical payments, secured or unsecured, and lump sum for spouses and children of the family on proof simply of failure to provide reasonable maintenance. Again, section 27 provides a means of obtaining orders for financial relief without issuing decree proceedings. However, it is another provision that is little used, despite the fact that the range of orders is wider than under the D.P.M.C.A.

Financial and property awards - section 15 of the Children Act 1989

Section 15 of the Children Act provides for the grant of a range of orders for the benefit of a child. The applicant must be a parent of guardian of the child and the orders can be made against a parent.

Orders depend on parenthood not marriage. The nature of the orders possible under the CA is discussed further on in the book..

Unmarried Partners

This section relates to spouses who do not seek a decree and to partners who have never been married to each other. In relation to the former, the following rights are important where divorce is not contemplated, or where a spouse has become insolvent or died. With cohabitees, the Matrimonial Causes Act does not apply. so these are their only rights with regard to joint property. The only difference between the two classes is that cohabitees have to prove to the courts that they had a settled relationship that was intended to be permanent.

Establishing a trust

When dealing with land there will always be documentary evidence as to ownership-the title deeds. It may be that both parties own the land or just one. However, in some case of joint ownership this is not spelt out. Here there is a rebuttable presumption that the legal owners are each entitled to an equal share of the beneficial estate. Further, the legal estate in the home may be vested in the sole name of one of the cohabitees. Here, there is a rebuttable presumption that the beneficial interest also belongs exclusively to that person.

In both these situations consideration of the title deeds alone will not necessarily provide the answer to an ownership dispute. Extrinsic evidence to rebut the presumptions can be adduced, evidence of the existence of a trust behind the deeds. Trusts are generally categorised as express, implied, resulting and constructive. Express trusts are not common in the family context. The other trusts, or distinctions are of little relevance. What is of relevance is the circumstances in which the court will accept that the trust has arisen, whether resulting, implied or constructive.

Payment towards the purchase price

Where one party provides the whole or the part of the purchase price for property that is conveyed into another persons name, there is a rebuttable presumption that the first party intended that he should benefit and the second party should hold the property on trust for him, either exclusively or in part, i.e. the beneficial estate "results" in whole or in part, to A. The trust is therefore known as a resulting trust. The concept of resulting trust is rarely directly applicable in the family context because usually the home is not purchased outright but by way of mortgage.

Two cases in the House of Lords Petit v. Petit (1969) and Gissing V.Gissing (1979) serve to highlight the complicated area of trusts. Both cases concerned a spouse who did not have an interest in the legal estate in the home claiming to be entitled to a beneficial interest by way of trust. There was a unanimous decision in both cases that a trust could arise where both parties had intended that it should. The court should look for a common intention that both parties should be beneficially entitled (common intent).

Proof of conduct from which the court can infer the common intent is not sufficient. The woman (in these cases) must also prove that she has acted "to her detriment or significantly altered her position in reliance on the common intent" before a trust in her favour will arise. Therefore, before such a trust can be established, the courts will scrutinise the parties conduct for two reasons: the first to ascertain that there was the common intent; the second to ascertain that the woman has acted upon it. The crucial questions are then seen to be what sort of conduct will give rise to the inference of common intent and what sort of conduct will show that the woman has acted upon it?

The most recent and authoritative statements on these issues are to be found in the leading judgment of Lord Bridge in Lloyds Bank PLC v. Rosset. Express discussions between the parties as to their interests in the property do not amount to conduct from which a common intent can be inferred. What is looked for are:

" direct contributions to the purchase price by the partner who is not the legal owner, whether initially or by payment of mortgage installments". These "will readily justify the inference necessary to the creation of a constructive trust. But...it is extremely doubtful whether anything less will do".

An express agreement

Where there is evidence of the parties having entered into "an agreement, arrangement or understanding that the property is to be shared beneficially" then, in some circumstances, the court will hold that a trust has arisen. The finding of such an agreement can only be based upon express discussions between the parties.

However, proving an agreement is not the end of the matter. The woman has to show, as before, that she has acted to her detriment or significantly altered her position in reliance on the agreement before the court will hold that a trust in her favour has arisen.

Two points need to be made in relation to this type of trust. First, it can be distinguished from an express trust, which does not require an agreement between the parties, nor the woman having acted to her detriment. Second, it can be distinguished from a trust arising from the common intention of the parties, because the court does not infer an agreement. Direct evidence of it must be present.

Again, the crucial issue is the sort of conduct that will be required before, for this type of trust, the woman will be held to have acted to her detriment.

Quantification of beneficial interests under a trust

In the past few years, there have been a number of cases concerning the quantification of shares. Where the cases concern a resulting trust, the shares are determined in relation to each party's contribution. Where the case concerns a trust arising from an express agreement of the parties or a trust arising from their common intent, as inferred from their conduct, the shares are determined by reference to that agreement or, if there is none, their common intent. Where there is no common agreement, the court is entitled to look at:

"all the circumstances surrounding the acquisition of the property, things said and done then and subsequently" including "their respective financial contributions to the purchase price. (B v B H.C. 1988). "the contributions which in total each had made. Those contributions would include, in addition to the original contribution, sums contributed to discharge of the ... mortgage and the cost of capital improvements." (Passee v. Passee (C.A. 1988).

Proprietary Estoppel

Estoppel is the principle that prevents a person from exercising or asserting his legal rights and usually the principle can only be pleaded in defence of an action to exercise or assert those rights. Proprietary estoppel, however, can only be used to assert contrary rights. The circumstances in which such a situation will be recognised by law are rigorously defined. In Coombes v. Smith (H.C. 1987) the court stated that a claim to a share in the beneficial interest of a property based upon proprietary estoppel would only succeed if the claimant can show:

(a) that she had made a mistake as to her legal rights in the property
(b) that she had spent money or done some other legal act as a result of that mistake
(c) that the defendant knew of his own rights in the property inconsistent with those she had
(d) that he knew of her mistaken belief
(e) that he encouraged her to act as above.

Occupation of the home

If a woman is successful in establishing that she has a beneficial interest in the property, she may then be faced with a demand that nevertheless the property be sold so that the man may at least realise his share. This could equally happen to a woman who is a joint owner on the face of the deeds. An immediate sale of the home can cause hardship.

By the Law of Property Act 1925 s30 the court can order the sale of the property subject to a trust for sale. But it can also refuse to make such an order. Generally it will do so if it is satisfied that the purpose of the trust is still unfulfilled. Thus if the home was in reality bought as a home for the family, it is likely that any application for the sale of the home prior to the children reaching majority age will be refused, despite the breakdown of marriage. Thus there is protection for the woman here, to some extent.

Because of the facts of their relationship the woman may not be able to establish that they own a share of the property. As a last resort, such a woman may be at least able to establish a right to occupy a home after the relationship has broken down.

This may be possible if the circumstances show that he has granted her a licence to stay on his property, a licence that was given for consideration and cannot be revoked by giving notice but only in accordance with the contract.

Courts are often asked to infer the granting of such licences. In Tanner v. Tanner (C.A. 1975) because the woman gave up a protected tenancy to go and live with the man and their children at his house, the court inferred the grant of a licence to occupy until his children left school. However, in Coombes v. Smith the court rejected the alternative claim of the plaintiff for a licence for the duration of her life.

The inference of a licence of this kind is based on the facts of each case and can be an extremely artificial exercise.

Chapter 6

Provision for Children

The Child Support Agency, was brought into being by the Child Support Act 1991. The purpose of the agency was to improve on the then existing child maintenance system that, according to the government allowed errant fathers to avoid maintenance with no real sanctions. The Government stated:

"The present system is unnecessarily fragmented, uncertain in its results, slow and in effective. It is largely based on discretion. The cumulative effect is uncertainty and inconsistent decisions about how much maintenance should be paid".

The C.S.A eventually came into force on April 5th 1993. The agency is responsible for all new cases, cases where the claimant is on income support and family credit. In 1995, in response to further criticism, the government introduced further legislation in the 1995 Child Support Act. The principle of the C.S.A. is that whatever the changes in parents relationships, they cannot change their responsibility towards their children. There is a formula laid out which fixes maintenance levels and Child Support Officers have wide powers to collect information.

The C.S.A applies to a "qualifying Child" defined by section 3(1) of the Act as a child where one or both of his parents is an "absent" parent. This means a parent who is not living in the same household as the child, notwithstanding contact arrangements. The person with whom the child has a home is called 'a person with care'. The Act only applies to children aged sixteen or under or nineteen or under and in full time education.

The C.S.A applies only to natural or adoptive parents or persons treated as parents under the H.F.E.A (Human Fertilisation and Embryology Act 1990). The absent parent is required to make periodical payments in accordance with fixed criteria.

Determining the father

Determining the natural father may require proof of paternity. Under the CSA 1991, s27, an application can be made for declaration of paternity. Courts can order that a blood test be taken and the test that will be applied is whether making such an order would be in the 'best interests' of the child. However, since the introduction of the Child Support, Pensions and Social Security Act 2000, s15, the Child Support Agency may now automatically assume the non-resident parent to be the father of the child if he was married to the mother at some stage between conception and birth; he is registered as the father; or he refuses to take scientific (for example DNA) tests.

Non-disclosure by the resident parent

Many women do not want to set in motion a process that will lead to the tracing of absent non-resident fathers.. The CSA 1991, s46(3) gives authorization for the disclosure requirement to be waived if there are reasonable grounds to believe that compliance would lead to risk to the claimant or child. If there are no reasonable grounds penalties can be imposed on the claimant. These penalties are in the form of reduced benefits. Penalties are also imposed on women who refuse to undergo the blood test to establish paternity.

Maintenance requirement

The C.S.A. lays down a maintenance requirement, the amount needed to maintain the child based on income support criteria. There is a maintenance assessment that is the assessable income of the absent parent, adding the income of person with care and dividing by two. There is also an additional element whereby the absent parent can be called upon to contribute further up to a statutory maximum. There is also a protected income level that is designed to ensure that the absent parent is better off than he would be on income support.

Once the assessment is made, the Agency may carry out collections and enforcement and will automatically do so where the claimant is on income support.

The Agency may make deductions from earnings orders under S31, and may apply to the Magistrates for a liability order under S33, and in the event of willful refusal or culpable neglect, imprisonment for up to six weeks under section 40.

S9(1) states that no agreement for maintenance can prevent a person with care from applying for an assessment and any clause purporting to exclude that right is void.

The maintenance assessment can only be made on application to the agency, but in respect of persons with care on benefit, they must authorise action on penalty of a reduction in benefit under section 46(5) of 20% for 26 weeks followed by 10% for a further year. Under s6(2) the requirement to co-operate may be waived if an officer is satisfied that there is a risk to a claimant or any child of, suffering harm or distress.

Maintenance assessments and special cases

Regulations 1992 give relief to an absent parent who has regular contact with his child. The assessment is reduced if the child spends 104 nights or more each year with the absent parents. Since April 1995, recognition has been given to take account of the need of the absent parent who had transferred capital, usually in the form of the matrimonial home, to the parent with care. This has been achieved by giving the absent parent a further allowance calculated ratably according to the value of the property transferred. The 1995 Act sought to incorporate greater flexibility into the scheme, by means of a series of departure directions which the secretary of state may influence if two conditions are fulfilled: the case falls within one or more of the cases set out in part 1 of schedule 4; and it is his opinion that it would be just and equitable to give the departure direction.

The overall effect will be to permit the agency to take account of certain circumstances, such as additional expenses borne by the absent parent, the fact that the absent parent has transferred property to the parent with care or that the parent with care is not utilising an asset to maximise its income producing potential so as to reduce the maintenance assessment which would otherwise be payable. The additional expenses include:

-costs incurred in long distance traveling to work;
-costs incurred by an absent parent in maintaining contact with the child;
-debts incurred before the parent became an absent parent in relation to the child. Though 'debts' are not defined, certain debts are excluded, including gambling debts, trade or business debts or use of credit cards;
-pre-1993 commitments which it is impossible, or it would be unreasonable to expect the parent concerned to withdraw from;
-costs incurred by a parent in supporting a child who is not his, but is part of his family.

Each are subject to rigorous conditions before it can qualify for consideration.

Few would argue with the CSA that parents are financially responsible for their children but the lack of flexibility in the calculation, the absence of appeals and the disregard for previous arrangements have caused exceptional hardship for some parents who have second families or who have made clean break settlements prior to the introduction of the CSA.

Although the C.S.A. supplants the courts powers, the sections of the Matrimonial Causes Act 1973 and Children's Act 1989 are not repealed and the provisions are still relevant. Courts have a role in the following circumstances:

a) Where the absent parent is sufficiently wealthy to be able to top up the maximum maintenance under the CSA.
b) Where the child is receiving full time instruction or training requiring provision of some or all of the expenses, e.g. school fees.
c) Where the child is disabled, orders may be made to meet some or all of the expenses attributable to that disability.
d) Where 17 and 18 year olds are not in full time education.
e) Where there is a lump sum or transfer of property order.
f) Where the child is a "child of the family" and not a qualifying child.

Matrimonial Causes Act 1973, as amended by the Matrimonial and Family Proceeding Act 1984.

Within the framework of the above children can have the same types of orders made in their favour, against either of the parties to the marriage as can the parties themselves. The order can direct payment to the child or third party. Generally, no application for an order in favour of a child over 18 can be made. Periodical payments orders secured or unsecured must terminate when the child reaches 17 unless the court decides to the contrary. Both types of payments must cease on the death of the payer.

Matters taken into account when making an order

As with spouse orders, the first consideration of the court, when deciding whether and how to exercise it powers, is the welfare of any minor children of the family. The courts, under M.C.A. s 25(3) will have regard to:

a) the financial needs of the child
b) the income, earning capacity, property and other financial resources of the child
c) any physical or mental disability of the child
d) the type of education or training he was receiving or was expected to receive by the parties to the marriage
e) the financial assets and needs of the parties, the standard of living enjoyed by the family prior to the breakdown of the marriage and any physical or mental disability of the parties.

The M.C.A. s 25(4) provides further factors to be taken into account when the court is considering making an order against a party to the marriage who is not a parent of the child, and include, for example the liability of any other person to maintain the child.

The Children Act 1989, Section 15

Section 15 of the CA provides for the grant of a range of financial and property awards for children subject to the C.S.A. The applicant must be the parent or guardian of the child and orders can be made against the parent.

It must be remembered that the availability of these orders is not dependent upon the parties being married to each other, it is dependent upon parenthood. However, married parents may make use of section 15 where there is no pending divorce proceedings.

The court has the power to make the following orders:

a) that either parent pay periodical payments for the benefit of the child, secured or unsecured
b) that either parent pay a lump sum for the benefit of the child
c) that either parent transfer property to which he is entitled to the child
d) that either parent do settle such property for the benefit of the child.

Payments and transfer for the benefit of the child can be ordered to be made direct to the child or to some third party. It should be noted that if applications are made to magistrates courts, the only orders that can be made are ones for unsecured periodical payments and lump sums not exceeding £1,000.

All the above orders benefit children alone. Orders for unsecured periodical payments cease on the death of the payer and for both types of periodical payments the rules for cessation when the child reaches a specific age apply.

The CA schedule one lists the matters that the court must take into account when deciding what order to make. They bear some similarity to those listed in the M.C.A. s 25(3), the factors relevant for child orders ancillary to decree proceedings.

Chapter 7

Domestic Violence

Definition of domestic violence

The Family Law Act 1996, does not refer to domestic violence as such, but to the concepts of molestation and harm. The courts have accepted the discretionary definition of molestation, which is to 'cause trouble, to vex, to annoy, to put to inconvenience' (Vaughn v Vaughn 1973)

Harm is defined in s63(1) Family law Act 1996:

i) in relation to an adult: ill treatment or the impairment of health
ii) for a child: ill treatment or impairment of health or development (physical, social, emotional or educational;
iii) includes sexual abuse and forms of ill treatment which are not physical.

The Adoption and Children Act 2002 adds into that definition harm caused by 'seeing or hearing violence perpetrated upon another' a recognition of the emotional harm caused to children who witness domestic violence.

Violence in the family is a common occurrence and can cause a great deal of misery to the victim of that violence. Although violence is not just physical but mental too, it is an unfortunate fact that much of the incidence of domestic violence is by men against women. Physical violence is a criminal offence. However, the criminal law is concerned primarily with punishment and does not take any steps to protect the victim. This section is concerned with civil remedies, mainly the injunction. An injunction can be granted to restrain violence and also molestation.

Horner v. Horner (1983) defined molestation as "any conduct which can properly be regarded a such a degree of harassment as to call for the intervention of the court". There are cases where an injunction restraining such behaviour will not be sufficient protection. In these case there can be no real alternative but to make an order separating the parties, an order which ousts one of them from the home.

These orders, ouster orders have many variations, for example, to prevent one party using certain rooms in the house or an ouster from the house or even the area.

Most commonly the woman seeks an order against the man. The powers can equally be used by man against woman.

Inherent Jurisdiction

By section 37(1) of the Supreme Courts Act 1981, the High Court is given the power to grant injunctions "in all cases in which it appears to be just and convenient to do so". This power is also given to the county court by section 38 of the County Courts Act 1984.

In the family law sphere, this power is frequently used to grant non-molestation injunctions as a part of a divorce suit. An injunction under these Acts can only be granted in support of a legal or equitable right.

It is accepted that everyone has a right not to be subjected to assault and battery and this has been relied upon by the courts, expressly or impliedly, when granting a wife a non-molestation injunction against her violent husband, as part of divorce proceedings. It is possible, however, that such injunctions are too wide.

In the case Patel v. Patel (1988) an injunction restraining the respondent from "assaulting, molesting or otherwise interfering or communicating with the applicant" had been granted to an unmarried woman as part of an action alleging trespass to the person. It was redrawn by the court to restrain, assault and molestation only. This was ordered on the basis that there is no right not to be harassed that could be supported by the words "otherwise interfering or communicating with".

Ouster injunctions present a different problem. Since Richards v. Richards, applications for ouster orders between spouses have to be made under the Matrimonial Homes Act. In practice, they may still be dealt with as part of the divorce proceedings but the Court must apply the principles of the M.H.A. in arriving at their decision. There have been conflicting decisions in the court of appeal concerning the power to grant ouster orders in proceedings concerning children.

In Ashbury v. Millington (1986) the court said it had no powers under the guardianship of Minors Act 1971, nor was there the power under the inherent jurisdiction. This was affirmed by F (minors) (Parental Home: Ouster) (1993) where a mother argued that her father should be excluded from the house so that she could live there with the children. She relied on the inherent jurisdiction and in the alternative, a CA, section 8 specific issue order. Her appeal was dismissed. An injunction under the inherent jurisdiction was not available and section 8 orders could not affect the fathers right of occupation. Finally, the injunction must bear a sensible relationship to the proceedings in which it is sought.

The Family Law Act 1996 Part 1V

Part 1V was implemented on October 1, 1997 and repeals a number of provisions in former Acts, notably the Matrimonial Homes Act 1983 and the Domestic Violence and Matrimonial Proceedings Act 1976. The Law Commission made several proposals in order to bring together all of the former provisions, which were considered highly unsatisfactory, and these are now codified in part 1V.

Associated persons or relevant child

In determining whether a client will be able to obtain a non molestation order under the Family Law Act 1996 the first matter to be ascertained is whether the applicant and respondent are "associated" within the meaning of the Act or, where the person sought to be protected is a child, whether the child is a "relevant "child.

The list of associated persons appears in s. 62 (4) and (5) of the Act and covers persons who, prior to the 1996 Act could not obtain injunctive relief unless they were able to rely upon behaviour which was capable of amounting to a tort or threatened tort and so bring a civil action to which injunctive relief might attach.

Persons are associated with each other if:

(a) they are married;
(b) they have been married;
(c) they are cohabitants;
(d) they are former cohabitants;
(e) they live in the same household;
(f) they have lived in the same household;
(g) they are relatives;
(h) they have agreed to marry each other;
(I) they are parents of the same child;
(j) they have, or have had, parental responsibility for the same child;
(k) they are parties to the same family proceedings.

The exception to this is where one of the parties is a body corporate (local authority).

Not only may they make their own application but they may include in the order a 'relevant child', that is:
-any child who is living with, or might reasonably be expected to live with either of the parents;

-any child in relation to whom an order under the Adoption Act 1976 or the C.A. is in question in the proceedings;
-any other child whose interests the court considers relevant.

Children under 16 can apply for an order with leave and if of sufficient understanding. Under C.A. amendments a parent may be removed from the home instead of taking a child into local authority care.

Non-Molestation Orders

Section 42 of the F.L.A. allows the court to make orders prohibiting a person from molesting a person with whom he is associated and from molesting a relevant child. The order may refer to molestation in general or particular acts of molestation or both, and may be made for a specified period or until further order. In exercising its discretion the court shall have regard to all the circumstances including the need to secure the health, safety and well being of the applicant or of any relevant child. There is no definition of molestation in the F.L.A. so all existing case law remains relevant.

Occupation orders

The Family Law Act attempts to simplify matters by granting courts the power to make a single order in relation to the home. The order is known as an occupation order. They replace ouster orders and are available to 'associated persons'.

There is a distinction drawn, in Section 33 of the F.L.A. between what are known as "non-entitled applicants and "entitled" applicants. Entitled applicants have a legal or beneficial interest in the home, non-entitled applicants do not.

Non-entitled applicants can only apply for orders against former spouses, cohabitants or former cohabitants.

An order under Section 33 may:
-enforce the applicants entitlement to enter and or remain in occupation of the house or even part of it;
-prohibit, suspend or restrict the exercise by the respondent of any right of his to occupy the home, including his matrimonial home rights;
-regulate the occupation of the dwelling house by either or both parties.

The courts powers

In deciding whether, and if so, how to exercise its powers the court must have regard to all the circumstances of the case, including:
-the housing needs and housing resources of the parties and of any relevant child:
-the financial resources of any of the parties;
-the likely effect of any order, or of a decision not to make an order, on the health, safety and well being of either party or relevant child or;
-the conduct of the parties in relation to each other or otherwise.

The balance of harm test

The court has complete discretion to make an order except under section 33(7) of the FLA. If it appears to the court that the applicant or any relevant child is likely to suffer any significant harm, attributable to conduct of the respondent if an order is not made, the court shall make the order unless it appears to it that the respondent or any relevant child is likely to suffer significant harm if the order is made, and that harm is as great or greater than the harm which is likely to be suffered by the applicant or child if the order is not made.

Applicant is a former spouse, a cohabitant or a former cohabitant with no existing right to occupy

Section 35 of the FLA applies if a former spouse is entitled to occupy a dwelling by virtue of a beneficial estate, etc, and the other former spouse is not so entitled: and the house was at any time their matrimonial home or was at any time intended by them to be their matrimonial home. For the purposes of this section, a person claiming an equitable interest in the home is deemed not to have a right to occupy.

Sections 36 and 37 of the Act make similar provisions for cohabitants and ex cohabitants who also do not have rights to occupy the former family home. Where the applicant is a former spouse, the court shall have regard not only to the matters set out in section 33\96\0 but also:

-the length of time that has elapsed since the parties ceased to live together;
-the length of time that has elapsed since the marriage was dissolved or annulled or;
-the existence of any pending proceedings between the parties for property adjustment orders under sections 23(a) or 24 of the M.C.A., or orders for financial relief under the C.A. or relating to the ownership of the dwelling home.

Where the applicant is a habitant or a cohabitant with no entitlement to occupy, additional circumstances to be taken into account are:
-the nature of parties to the relationship;
-the length of time during which they have lived together as husband and wife;
-whether there are or have been any children who are children of both parties or for whom they have or have had parental responsibilities.

The terms of the orders are the same as those available under section 33 of the FLA but the duration of the orders will differ. An order in respect of former spouses:

-may not be made after the death of either of the former spouses; and
-ceases to have effect on either of them;
-must be limited so as to have effect for a specified period not exceeding six months, but may be extended on one or more occasions for a further specified period not exceeding six months.

Applicant is a spouse, former spouse, a cohabitant or former cohabitant and neither applicant nor respondent has a right to occupy

Sections 37 and 38 of the F.L.A. deal with these situations, which are likely to be rare in practice. They deal with persons who occupy their home under contract with their employers or live in home owned by their parents, for example. Whatever their circumstances, the court is empowered to make orders in the same terms as under section 33 of the F.L.A.

Additional powers

Section 40(1)(a) of the Act provides that the court may, on making an order under ss 33, 35 or 36-or at any time thereafter-impose on either party obligations as to:

-the repair and maintenance of the dwelling house
-the discharge of rent
-the discharge of mortgage payments
-the discharge of other outgoings affecting the dwelling house.

It is anticipated that this power will be particularly useful when an occupation order continues for some time or while the outcome of the proceedings under the Matrimonial Causes Act 1973 is awaited.

The Law Commission also suggested that the court should have power to order an occupying party to make payments to the other for that occupation. Under the old law only the non-entitled spouse could be ordered to make such payments.

The Protection from Harassment Act 1997

This Act came into force on June 18th 1997. Although it is intended as a remedy against stalking, it is sufficiently wide to cover domestic situations as well. Section 1 provides that a person must not pursue a course of conduct that amounts to harassment of another and which he knows, or to know, amounts to harassment.

Section 2 creates a summary offence and section 4 an indictable offence where a person is put in fear of violence. The courts are empowered, in addition to other punishment, to issue restraining orders forbidding the offender from doing anything specified by the order for the purpose of protecting the victim. Further, section 3 creates a statutory tort of harassment and provides for the issue of injunctions, the breach of which entitles the plaintiff to apply for a warrant to arrest the defendant.

It is possible that this Act may be used to bypass non-molestation orders under the F.L.A. 1996 and injunctions under the inherent jurisdictions as well as being available to those who are not 'associated' with the defendant.

Enforcement

The matter of enforcement of these orders is always difficult. It is one thing to obtain an order and another to ensure that it is enforced.

In many cases, such orders are broken, and the topic of how to enforce obedience to such orders is very important indeed.

No court can directly force respondents to comply with such orders. Applicants must rely on the court's powers to punish respondents and hope that this, or the threat of it, will force compliance. Breach of an injunction granted either by the High Court or County Court is contempt and is punishable by either a fine or imprisonment.

To obtain the punishment of the respondent by either of these two methods, the applicant must take the responsibility for the institution and continuation of the process, a factor that can cause great stress and anxiety.

To avoid this, and the incurring of further costs by employing a solicitor, a power of arrest can be attached to injunctions and orders. The effect of this is that the police can arrest, without warrant, a person who has breached the order. The only initiative the applicant must take is to contact the police following the breach. The police must bring the person before the relevant court within 24 hours and the court can impose penalty.

As the arrest of an offender has dire consequences, the power of arrest attached to an order is usually hedged by limitations.

Domestic Violence, Crime and Victims Act 2004

New legislation has recently come into force as above, which has attempted to bridge the gap between the criminal and civil law relating to domestic violence. It inserts a new s 42A into the family Law Act 1996 and makes it a criminal offence to flout the civil orders relating to non-molestation, even where there is no power of arrest relating to the order. The Act makes common assault an arrestable offence, provides greater protection to victims during court hearings, improves sentencing of those convicted, establishes multi-agency reviews after familial killings, creates a register of offenders and aims to ensure that criminal and civil courts dealing with domestic violence liaise with each other.

Chapter 8

Children And Adults

Parents Rights and obligations

Definition of a parent
The actual legal definition of a parent has been the subject of debate over the years. Whether the parent is a biological parent or psychological parent.

Biological parents
The law has traditionally approached the question of parentage by considering the biological link between adult and child as preferable. The law will rarely interfere with the authority of the biological parent, unless some other arrangement is preferable. In Re KD (a minor) (Ward: termination of access) 1988, Lord Templeman stated:

'The best person to bring up a child is the natural parent. It matters not whether the parent is wise or foolish, rich or poor, educated or illiterate, providing the child's moral and physical health is not endangered'.

There are two exceptions to this presumption: where the child is adopted (Adoption Act 1976 s39) and secondly where reproduction and childbirth follows on from sperm or egg donation (Human Fertilisation and Embryology Act 1990 s27-28). Adoption will terminate the legal (parental) responsibility of natural parents towards the child and also extinguishes any rights a parent may have over a child. Where a person donates genetic material (eggs, sperm, embryos) he relinquishes any rights to biological parentage in relation to any child that may be born as a result.

Psychological parents

Good parenting depends very much on the ability to form an emotional/psychological bond with a child. A strong attachment between parent and child is considered to be and indicator of a stable and emotionally healthy relationship.

This bond is not exclusive to the biological parent but can form with a number of people, such as foster and adoptive parents. The courts have recognised the possibility of the independence of the biological and psychological relationship.

Parenting and the changing social context

During the last 50 years or so the family has undergone significant changes with respect to public perception and also the law. A number of aspects of the family need to be considered: socially acquired parentage, sexual orientation and parentage and multi-cultural family arrangements. With regard to socially acquired parentage, this refers to step-parents, a situation which will arise through either divorce or one-parent families resulting in remarriage. It can be said that the step parent will acquire the mantle of mother or father, with their role far more significant than the actual biological absent parent.

With regard to sexual orientation, whilst the heterosexual family remains the norm, homosexual men will father children and lesbian women will give birth to babies. They would also be considered parents. The assumption that homosexuals are not fit parents was challenged in Re W (Adoption: Homosexual Adopter) 1997, in which Singer J held that there was nothing in the Adoption Regulations to prevent a homosexual adopting a child and allowed a 49 year old lesbian woman in a settled relationship to adopt. The Adoption and Children Act 2002 (see adoption) has now authorised adoption by homosexual men and women.

With regards to multi-cultural family arrangements, patterns of immigration over the last 50 years have changed the family make up of the United Kingdom. In addition, the cultural make up of the country has changed and with it a need by the law to recognise and accept different cultural traditions.

The legal parent

A parent, in the eyes of the law is a person who has responsibility for a child. Parental responsibility means 'all the rights, duties, powers, responsibilities and authorities which by law a parent has in relation to the child and his property' (Children Act 1989 s3). Legal parenthood carries the right and responsibility to register a child's name within six months of its birth and apply for residence/contact orders, specific issue orders, change the child's name and to apply for a prohibited steps order to prevent the removal of the child from the country.

A parent is the natural mother or natural father of the child. However, not all fathers have parental responsibility for their child and other parties may also have parental responsibility for the child. In addition, the local authority may have parental responsibility for the child where the child is in care, and foster parents may have responsibility. More than one person can have parental responsibility for a child (CA 1989 s 2(5)). Where other parties have parental responsibility for the child, this will only last for the duration of the order made in their favour.

Parental responsibility

Any person who is a legal parent has parental responsibility. In accordance with the Children Act 1989, s2, more than one person may have responsibility for the child at any one time. Thus, parental responsibility is shared in the case of a married couple and is shared where parents are separated. In cases where children are taken into care, the natural parents will still have parental responsibility: the responsibility will simply be shared with foster parents.

The following outlines who has parental responsibility:
- The mother has automatic parental responsibility (whether a child is born within or out of marriage);
- The married father;
- The unmarried father has automatic responsibility if the Adoption and Children Act 2002 s111(2)(a)(c) applies;
- The unmarried father if he is granted a court order under the Children Act 1989, s4;
- The adoptive parents of an adoptive child;
- If a child is a ward of court the court stands in the position of parents and a court in wardship has parented responsibility;
- A guardian appointed by a parent by deed or will has parental responsibility after the parents death;
- The Children's Act 1989 created the institution of custodianship, under which many parental rights are given to the foster parent but some rights remain with the natural parent.

Proving parentage
In cases where the identity of the biological father is unknown and the mother wishes to establish parentage, or the child or father wishes to dispute parentage, an order for a declaration of paternity (under the Family Law Act) 1986, s55A, as amended by the Child Support, Pensions and Social Security Act 2000, s83(2) may be made. However, blood testing will only be ordered if it is considered to be in the child's

best interests. In re O; Re J (children) (Blood Tests: Constraint) (2000) in two separate cases, a male applicant had obtained an order under s 20 (1) of the Family Law Reform Act 1969 for the use of blood tests designed to determine the paternity of a child who was the subject of the proceedings. In each case, the mother, whose consent was required under s 21(3) of the 1969 Act, refused to consent to the child's blood being tested. The court held that it was a matter for the mother to grant or withhold consent.

The courts, however, can order a blood test to be taken if it considers this to be in the best interests of child.

Step-parents

Where a parent remarries, the new spouse becomes the step-parent of any children of the previously married partner. Under the Adoption and Children's Act 2002, amending the Children's Act 1989 s 4(A)1:

Where a child's parent (A) who has parental responsibility for the child is married to a person who is not the child's parent (step parent) (a) parent A or, if the other parent of the child also has parental responsibility for the child, both parents may, by agreement with the step-parent provide for the step-parent to have parental responsibility for the child or (b) the court may, on application of the step-parent, order that the step-parent shall have parental responsibility for the child.

The Civil Partnership Act 2004 provides that civil partners will be eligible to apply for parental responsibility on the same basis as step parents.

Adoptive parents

An order of the court placing a child for adoption establishes the adoptive parent as the legal parent. The ACA 2002, s 46(1) states:

1) an adoption order is an order made by the court on an application under s 50 or 51 giving parental responsibility for a child to the adopters or adopter.

2) The making of an adoption order operates to extinguish the parental responsibility which any person other than the adopters or adopter has for the adopted child immediately before the making of the order.

Foster parents

When a child is in care of the local authority, he or she will be placed with foster carers. This can be a single adult or an adult couple in a family arrangement.

Parents and reproductive technology

As mentioned in the introduction to this book, there is a new Human Fertilisation and Embryology Bill making its way through Parliament. This is in its early stages and will likely take a while before it becomes law.

Under the current Human Fertilisation and Embryology Act (HFEA) 1990, where person has donated sperm or eggs then he or she relinquishes any rights over the genetic material. The HFEA determines the legal parent as a result of a child born from IVF treatment. THE HFEA 1990, s 27 defines a 'mother' as 'the woman who is carrying or who has carried a child as a result of the placing in her of an embryo, or of sperm or eggs'.

Section 28 defines a father as being married to the woman 'at the time of placing in her of an embryo or the sperm or the eggs or of her insemination' unless it is shown that he did not consent to the placing in her of the embryo, sperm or eggs or to her insemination.

Parties separating

When parties who consented to the placement of genetic material in the woman separate, a specific legal position arises. In the case of Re R (a child) (IVF Paternity of Child) 2005, the mother, A, and her partner B, were unmarried and sought IVF treatment which involved the fertilisation of A's eggs with sperm from a donor. In accordance with IVF procedure, B signed a form acknowledging that he would be the father of any child born in consequence. However, A and B had already separated when implementation in A had taken place, about which B had no knowledge. On an application by B, the judge declared under HFEA 1990, s28(3) that B was the legal father of the resulting child. The court of appeal allowed A's appeal. B appealed and the House of Lords dismissed the ruling of the court of appeal holding:

'that section 28(3) of the HFEA should only apply to cases falling clearly within it and the legal relationship of a parent should not be based on a fiction, especially where deception was involved: that the embryo had to have been placed in the woman when treatment services were provided for her and the man together; and that, although they had originally been so provided for A and B, they had not been when implementation took place'.

Meaning of parental responsibility

Parents have a responsibility to care for the child. This means the responsibility to determine the place and manner of the upbringing of the child. They also have a responsibility to ensure that the child receives full time education., whether by going to school or home tutoring.

Parents have no legal responsibility to bring a child up in any faith. The court will, however, be sensitive to issues concerning faith when dealing with child matters.

Rights to discipline children

Under common law, discipline of a child must not be 'for the gratification of passion'. In Re H (minors) (Wardship: Cultural background) 1987, the parents came from a different cultural background, but the court held that this was no defence to physical punishment and held:

' Where the court in discharge of its parental duties was dealing with children of foreign ethnic origins and culture it must consider the situation against the reasonable objective standards of that culture so long as they did not conflict with minimum acceptable standards of child care in England, and always provided that the one criterion on which its decision is based was the welfare and best interests of the children concerned'.

Judicially ordered punishment has been held to be degrading and corporal punishment is prohibited in state schools by the Education (No2) Act 1986 s 47. The United Nations Convention on the Rights of the Child 1989 also imposes obligations on member states in respect of protecting children from domestic violence.

Right to consent to medical treatment

Parental responsibility on caring for the child also extends to medical treatment. Failure to undertake this responsibility may be a criminal act. The Children's Act 1989 s35 states:

A person who:
    a) does not have parental responsibility for a particular child; but
    b) has care of the child

may, subject to the provisions of the act, do what is reasonable in all the circumstances of the case for the purpose of safeguarding or promoting the child's welfare.

Right to withhold consent for marriage

Parents have the right to withhold consent from a proposed marriage where the minor is 16-17 years of age.

Chapter 9

Adoption

The Adoption and Children Act 2002

The central objective of adoption is now aimed at providing a stable and permanent future in a family for children who are being cared for by the local authority. The new legislation has introduced some significant improvements to existing adoption law. The main aim is to ensure that the welfare of the child is paramount (ACA 2002 s 1(2). Courts must apply this test when considering an adoption order. Also, the courts can dispense with the consent of existing parents if the welfare of the child requires it.

The 2002 ACA also recognises the geopolitics of family life-that for many children maintaining contact with birth parents is of the utmost importance. With this in mind, ACA s1 (4) (f) requires courts to consider:

'the relationship the child has with relatives, and with any other person in relation to whom the court or agency considers the relationship to be relevant, including:

(i) the likelihood of any such relationship continuing and the value to the child of its doing so;

(ii) the ability and willingness of any of the child's relatives, or of any such person to provide the child with a secure environment in which the child can develop, and otherwise to meet the child's needs;

(iii) the wishes and feelings of any of the child's relatives, or of any such person, regarding the child.

This represents a significant departure from previous adoption law which was to sever all ties with the birth family. The ACA 2002 s 1(5) requires that in placing the child for adoption, the agency must give due consideration to the child's religious persuasion, racial origin and cultural and linguistic background. This is also a departure from earlier adoption law, which placed the emphasis on religion only.

Whilst working towards acquiring the consent of the natural parents to adoption remains a priority (ACA 2002 s19(1) dispensing with consent has now been simplified and is permitted if the welfare of the child requires it, or the natural parents cannot be found or are incapable of giving consent.

The ACA 2002 abolishes the freeing order and introduces a placement order which can only be made if the parents have consented or if their consent may be dispensed with.

The ACA 2002 recognises that contemporary families may not be monogamous or heterosexual. However, stability and permanence in a relationship is recognised as of paramount importance. Unmarried couples can now adopt. This also includes homosexual couples. Single persons can also adopt. However, a single homosexual man may not be seen as suitable as a single heterosexual.

In Frette v France 2003, a single homosexual man applied for prior authorization to adopt. His sexual orientation was a decisive factor in the courts refusal. The court took the view that the applicants lifestyle did not appear to be such as to provide sufficient guarantees that he would be able to provide a suitable home for the child.

Step-parents can now acquire parental responsibility through a 'parental order' rather than adoption.

The ACA 2002 also introduces a new status of 'special guardianship' where total severance from the birth family is not appropriate and the possibility of contact with birth parents pertains.

Once an adoption order is made, adoption is final. Adoption terminates, once and for all, the parental responsibility of the natural parent.

Adoption services

Under the ACA 2002, only a local authority or a registered adoption society can provide adoption services. The latter must be registered under the National Care Standards Commission. Under s4(1) of the act 'adoption agencies' have responsibility for selecting and assessing adopters and placing children for adoption. This includes the provision of support services, discussed below.

S5 states that local authorities must prepare a clear adoption plan for the provision of services with regard to the adoption of the child. Section 109 requires the court to draw up a plan with a view to determining applications.

Care plans

Where the local authority wishes to place a child for adoption, it is the duty of the local authority in all care cases to file a care plan. The care plan sets out the local authority's plans for the child's future. The local authority may take the view that adoption is the preferred option. If this is the case, it should advise the court of the likely steps and timescales.

Adoption of children from overseas

There are rules and procedures governing the adoption of children overseas. Anyone wishing to adopt a child from overseas must apply for an eligibility certificate' from a casework team at the Department of Education.

Who can adopt?

A person can only be adopted if he or she is under 19 years of age. The application must be made before the child is 18 years old. In practice, if a child is over 12 then removing a child from parents or foster parents may not be in the interests of the child. The local authority will usually look for other alternatives.

The new rules under the ACA 2002 s 50, provide that a heterosexual (married or unmarried) couple or homosexual couple may adopt provided that there is sufficient permanency in their relationship. Section 51 allows a single person to adopt, although this was the case under the Adoption Act 1976.

Suitability

ACA 2002 s45 specifies two grounds in assessing the suitability of adopters. In assessing suitability, the Act specifies:

- suitability and permanence of that relationship (s45(2);
- religious persuasion, racial origin and cultural and linguistic background (s1(5)).

In addition to the statutory grounds the adoption agency may have their own criteria. Under the Adoption Act 1976, adoption agencies developed their own views of relevant criteria beyond the bare minimum laid down in statute. Certain types of persons were specifically excluded, for example those with children of their own. Also excluded were those who held certain religious views or no views at all, smokers and those who were overweight. The dominant view was that a child should have a reasonable expectation of parental longevity. The local authority also put an age limit on those who wished to adopt, women at 35 and men at 40. Any person wishing to adopt must undergo an assessment. Adopter assessment details various aspects of the would be adopters home life; language spoken at home; religion; ethnic descent; occupation; current or proposed hours of work; the children in the household; their ethnic descent, type of school that they go to and their relationship to the applicant; family members personalities, interests, experiences; the neighbourhood, its composition, its schools and recreational facilities and public transport. The applicant has to provide a description of where the child will live and its make up. Information on whether the applicant will move house in the future is also required. The agency will also carry out an assessment of physical and mental health of the proposed adopter.

Matching parents and children

The ACA 2002 also places emphasis on the importance of religious persuasion, racial origin and cultural and linguistic background in the process of matching adoptive parents to children placed for adoption. It is recognised that perfect matching may not always be possible, in fact it will be impossible to match all the variables. In Re C (Adoption: Religious Observance (2002) a child of a mixed race background with Jewish, Irish Roman Catholic and Turkish Cypriot Muslim elements was placed for adoption with a Jewish couple. The guardian for the child issued proceedings arguing that the couple were too Jewish and that the child should be placed in a secular home. The court held that where a child's heritage was very mixed, it would rarely be possible for it all to be reflected in the identity of the adoptive home.

Regulation and review of decisions

The ACA 2002, s 45, provides for the regulation of agency decisions in respect of suitability. A system of review introduced by the Act ensures that what are called 'qualifying determinations' which are decisions that conclude that a prospective applicant is unsuitable, are subject to review. A system of review is established and decisions about suitability are subject to an independent review. Complaints can be made to the local authority.

Court orders

The two orders of the court with regard to adoption are:

- a placement order
- an adoption order

Placement order

A placement order is an order authorising a local authority to place a child for adoption where there is parental consent, or where there is no consent and consent can be dispensed with. The court can only make a placement order where the child is subject to a care order. Conditions for making a care order are met when the child has no parent or guardian and the parents have consented or their consent should be dispensed with.

If parents refuse consent the court can dispense with consent on two statutory grounds. The first ground (s52(2)(a)) is where the parent or guardian cannot be found or is incapable of giving consent. The second Ground (s52(2)(b)) is where the welfare of the child requires the consent to be dispensed with.

Adoption order

Under the ACA 2002 s 46, an adoption order is made by the court on an application under s 50 or s 51 giving parental responsibility for the child to adopters. These can be made by the high court, county court or magistrates court. No order can be made without the child attending the hearing, unless special circumstances exist. An adoption order gives parental responsibility to the adopters and the child is treated as if born to the adopters in marriage. Each parent/guardian must be joined as a respondent as well as the adoption agency or local authority which has care of the child. If the adoption is refused, the child must be returned to the adoption agency within seven days of the order. The court can make a short term order which gives the applicant parental responsibility for two years and not more. Conditions can be attached to the order.

Alternatives to adoption orders

The ACA 2002 s 1(6) requires the court to be satisfied that the order it makes is better than the alternative order or making no order at all. The court is required to consider all alternatives and will look to maintain links with the natural family.

Adoption by step-parents

The ACA 2000, s 39, provides for adoption by partners of parents. However, it is expected that fewer stepparents will apply for adoption as a parental responsibility order can also infer parental responsibility.

Discovery and information

The Registrar General is required to keep records so that it is possible to trace the original birth registration of an adopted person. The ACA 2002 provides no absolute right to birth records.

Human rights and genetic identity

Human rights legislation and the UNCRC 1989 reinforce the right of a child to know its genetic identity as follows:

Article 7: Each child should be registered immediately after birth, and has the right from birth to a name, to acquire a nationality, and as far as possible to know and to be cared for by his or her parents;

Article 8: Each child has the right to preserve his or her identity, including nationality, name and family relations, as recognised by law, without unlawful interference.

Article 9: Children should not be separated from their parents against their will, unless competent authorities which are subject to judicial review determine through the applicable legislation and procedures that such separation is necessary for the best interests of the child. All parties to such procedures shall be given the opportunity to participate in the proceedings and make their views known. A child separated from one or both parents has the right to maintain personal relations and direct contact with both parents on a regular basis, unless this is contrary to the child's interests. When separation results from state action such as detention, imprisonment, deportation or exile, the state shall provide essential information about the absent family on request, unless to do so would be detrimental to the child's well-being.

Chapter 10

Children and The Human Rights Act

The United Nations Convention on the rights of the child
The Convention transforms into legal obligations the affirmations on the Declaration of the Rights of the Child, which was adopted by the general assembly of the United Nations in 1959.

The Convention was ratified by the UK in 1991 but was taken into account when the Children Act 1989 was drafted. It is monitored by the Committee on the Rights of the Child, which makes suggestions and recommendation to governments and the general assembly on how the convention obligations can be met.

Definition of child
For the purposes of the UN Convention a child means, 'every human being below the age of 18 years unless, under the law applicable to the child, majority is attained earlier'. The preamble to the Convention talks about the protection of the child before and after birth, but the UK Government entered a reservation limiting the application of the convention to children born alive. This means the Convention does not, in the UK, give the right to life for a foetus.

Fathers have no right to act as advocate for the foetus, because the foetus is regarded as not having individual rights

The main rights given by the Convention

- Article 2 - all the rights apply to all children, without discrimination on the basis of their race, colour, sex,

language, religious, political or other opinion, national or social origin, property, disability, birth or other status.
- Article 3 - the best interest of the child shall be a primary consideration. The state is to provide adequate care when the family fails to do so.
- Article 6 - every child has an inherent right to life.
- Article 7 - every child has a right to a name from birth and to have a nationality
- Article 9 - a child has a right to live with his or her parents unless that is incompatible with his or her best interest, and the right to maintain contact with both parents if separated from them.
- Article 12 - the child has a right to express an opinion and have that opinion taken into account in accordance with his age and maturity.
- Article 13 - the child has a right to obtain and make known information and to express his or her views.
- Article 15 - children have a right to free association with others.
- Article 16 - they have a right to protection from interference with privacy, family, home and correspondence and from libel and slander.
- Article 18 - both parents have joint responsibility in bringing up their children and the state should support them in this task.
- Article 19 - the state has an obligation to protect children from all forms of maltreatment.
- Article 20 - the state has an obligation to provide special protection for children deprived of their family environment and to ensure an alternative family carer for them, taking into account their cultural background.

- Article 21 - adoption shall only be carried out in the best interest of the child,
- Article 22 - special protection is to be given to refugee children.
- Article 23 handicapped children are to receive special care, education and training to help them achieve the greatest possible self-reliance,
- Article 27 - children have a right to an adequate standard of living.
- Article 28-29 - they have a right to education and at least primary education should be free. Such education should be directed at developing the child's personality and talents, preparing the child for active life as an adult.
- Article 30 - children of minority communities and indigenous peoples have a right to enjoy their Own culture, religion and language.
- Article 31 - children have a right to leisure, play and participation in cultural activities.
- Article 32 - states must protect children from work which is a threat to their health, education or development.
- Article 33-36 - children have the right to be protected from drugs, sexual exploitation and abuse, trafficking and abduction and other forms of exploitation.
- Article 37 - no child shall be subjected to torture, cruel treatment, capital punishment, life imprisonment or unlawful deprivation of liberty
- Article 40 - child offenders have a right to due process of law.

The European Convention on Human Rights

The Human Rights Act 1998 incorporated, indirectly, the European Convention For the Protection of Fundamental Freedoms and Human Rights 1950 (ECHR) into UK law by requiring courts to interpret domestic law in a manner which is compatible with the convention. Accordingly, 'human rights' issues may be raised by parties within all family proceedings. The domestic courts are not now bound by precedent created before the HRA 1998, but may reinterpret old law to ensure it is now compatible with the Convention. As an alternative, individuals who believe that their human rights have been breached by a public authority which has acted in a way incompatible with the Convention may sue under s7 and s8 of the HRA 1998.

Freestanding human rights applications in family cases

Freestanding applications against a public authority involve a more detailed investigation of the balancing exercise undertaken in the decision-making process than the alternative remedy of judicial review In HRA 1998 applications to the court must assess whether:

- an article of the Convention is engaged;
- it has been interfered with;
- the interference is in accordance with the law, and that law is reasonably foreseeable and accessible;
- the interference is in pursuit of a legitimate aim that interference is 'necessary in a democratic society'. This means it must correspond to a 'pressing social need' and is a 'proportionate' response to the problem.

The more serious the intervention the more compelling must be the justification

If there are existing care proceedings, human rights issues should be raised within those proceedings as all tiers of the family court system have jurisdiction under HRA 1998. After care orders are made, the parents and children continue to have a right to respect for their family life. Allegations of interference at this stage can be made as a freestanding civil application, or an application can be made under the CA 1989 and the human rights issues raised in those proceedings

A Local Authorities failure to protect children

A public authority has a positive duty to ensure that the rights of individuals are secured, as well as ensuring that its own acts were not incompatible with the convention. The European Court has held that the failure of a local authority to take into care four children who then suffered serious neglect and abuse amounted to inhuman and degrading treatment Similarly, leaving children in a home where a convicted abuser was known to reside and who subsequently abused the children was a breach of Article 3. The local authority should have investigated and taken steps to stop the abuse happening and to manage the case properly.

Procedural rights

The right to respect for family life means that parents must be involved in decision making to a degree which is sufficient to offer adequate procedural protection for their interests The right to a fair trial includes the ability to take issues relating to your civil rights to court, not merely being afforded a fair process when you get there.

Although there may be circumstances in which parents allege breaches of their rights after a care order is made but there is no relevant application available under the CA 1989, this does not make the CA 1989 incompatible with the Convention because the matter can be dealt with by way of freestanding application under s7 and s8 HRA 1998. A fair trial does not just comprise fairness at the judicial stage but fairness throughout the litigation process, and all documents and meetings must be open to all parties Individuals must be given the opportunity to contest the reliability; relevance or sufficiency of the information being compiled on them.

Procedural safeguards continue after the litigation is over. If there is to be a change in a care plan, parents must be told of the proposed changes and given the opportunity to make representations and to challenge the evidence on which the changes are based. The local authority is under a duty to make full and frank disclosure of all relevant information. Procedural flaws may not be sufficiently severe to affect the outcome of the case and justify a local authority's decision being set aside. Unless there are justifiable reasons to the contrary, a father without parental responsibility should be given leave to be joined in applications relating to his child to secure respect for his family life. Other applicants for leave to make applications under s8 CA 1989, such as grandparents, may also have Article 6 and 8 rights, and the minimum essential protection of these rights is that judges must be careful not to dismiss the applications without full inquiry

Proportionality of response

The actions of a local authority must be proportionate to the current risk of harm to the child concerned. Action must not be excessive or arbitrary. The lowest-level protective mechanisms must be used first. So removal of a child from a mother who was not currently mentally ill and who was in the controlled environment of a hospital was unjustified.

The local authority must look at the type of harm alleged and at the timescale within which it is thought likely that the risk will come to fruition when choosing protective measures If a supervision order would work because there was a level of parental cooperation and the risk of harm was at the low end of the spectrum, a care order which gave the local authority parental responsibility when they did not need it would be a disproportionate response. Balancing conflicting human rights It may be necessary and proportionate to interfere with a parent's human rights to protect the human rights of a child, such as where granting a very late application by a father to be joined in proceedings would breach the child's right to a fair trial by causing undue delay.

In judicial decisions where the Article 8 rights of the parents and those of a child are at stake, the child's rights must be the paramount consideration. If any balancing of rights is necessary, those of the child must prevail

Chapter 11

Protection of Children and the Resolution of Disputes

A guardianship scheme was been created by the Children's Act ss 5 and 6 and a parental responsibility order for unmarried fathers. There are four orders created by s 8 of the Children's Act, Section 8 Orders:

1. Residence Order;
2. Contact Order;
3. A Prohibited Steps Order;
4. A Specific Issues Order.

Residence order

This is an order that settles the arrangements to be made as to the person with whom the child is to live. It can be made in favour of any person, with the exception of the local authority. It can be made in favour of more than one person specifying periods of time spent with individuals if they do not live together.

In many cases, the person with parental responsibility will be granted the order. However, it is the person to whom the order is granted who assumes responsibility.

Contact Order

This is an order requiring the person with whom the child resides to allow the child to visit or stay with another person. Again, local authorities are excluded.

Prohibited Steps Order

This is an order directing a person named in the order not to take any specified step in relation to the child without the permission of the court.

Specific Issues Order

This is an order that determines a specific question in connection with any aspect of parental responsibility. An example may mean schools attended, religion etc.

Section 8 orders can be made subject to directions as to their implementation and conditions that must be complied with. None of these orders can be made once a child has reached his 16th birthday or extend beyond then unless there are exceptional circumstances (s9(6) and (7).

Different types of proceedings

The only way for private individuals to take steps to resolve disputes concerning bringing up a child is for one of them to issue proceeding under the Children's Act. Like the above orders, the Children's Act has greatly simplified dispute resolution. The only exceptions to this relate to wardship and adoption.

Under the Children's Act it is possible to apply for an order appointing a guardian of the child (s 5). An order of this type gives parental responsibility. It is also possible for an unmarried father to apply far an order that gives him parental responsibility. The main type of application possible under the Children Act however, is a section 8 order.

An application for such an order can be made in several ways, either as a "free standing application" or as part of "family proceedings" Section 8 defines "family proceedings" The list includes jurisdictions which used to have their own powers to grant orders relating to upbringing of children, for example the M.C.A. It also includes applications under part one of the Children's Act itself. It should be noted that once family proceedings have commenced, the court can make a section 8 order itself, of its own motion.

Types of applicant
In most cases, it is the parents of the child who are in dispute about its upbringing. However, others with an interest in the child's welfare may also make an application. The Children Act recognises the need for persons other than parents of a child to be able to get orders that relate to the child's upbringing:

Those entitled to apply for any s 8 order:

1. A parent or guardian of the child;
2. A person who has been granted a residence order.

Those entitled to apply for a residence or contact order:
1. A spouse or ex spouse in relation to whom the child is a child of the family;
2. A person with whom the child has lived for at least three years. This need not be continuous as long as the period does not begin more than five years, nor end more than three months before, the making of the application;
3. A person who has the consent of the person in whose favour there is a residence order, if one has been granted, the local authority if the child is in care and in any other case any other person with parental responsibility.

The factors a court must take into account when considering making an order are designed to prevent applications deemed not to be serious and also possibly injurious to the child's future well-being. They include the nature of the persons connection with a child (s 10 (9).

Protection of Children-Local Authorities
Types of orders available

Before the Children's Act came into being, there were many types of orders available to local authorities which enabled them to offer some form of protection to children. Local authorities could, on passing a specific resolution, assume the role of parent.

The Children's Act makes an attempt to get rid of the uncertainty of the old laws. It replaced all the old laws and replaced them with a new scheme. In addition, local authorities can no longer pass a parental rights resolution. No child may be taken into care without a court order.

The following orders are available:

1. Care orders (s 31);
2. Supervision orders (s 31);
3. The Education supervision order (s 36);
4. The Emergency protection order (s 44);
5. The Child assessment order (s 43).

Care orders

This is an order that commits a child into the care of a local authority. It cannot be made in favour of anyone else. The effect of a care order is that the child in question goes to live in a local authority community home, or with local authority foster parents. The legal effect is that the local authority gains parental responsibility for the child while the order is in force. A care order automatically brings to an end any residence order that exists. But if a parent or guardian has parental responsibility at the time that a care order comes into force, this continues. A care order cannot be made in respect of a child who has reached 17 (16 if married). It lasts until the age of 18.

Supervision orders

This is an order placing the child under the supervision of a local authority or probation officer. This order does not carry any parental responsibility and there is no power to take a child from his home.

A supervision order can have conditions attached to it as the court sees fit. A supervision order cannot be made in respect of a child who has reached the age of 17 (16 if married). Generally, a supervision order has a life span of one year but can be extended to two years.

Education supervision orders

This is an order placing a child under the supervision of the local education authority.

Emergency protection orders

Orders usually take time to activate. For those children requiring emergency protection the above order is issued. It is an order that empowers the local authority or NSPCC to remove a child from its home and also gives the local authority parental responsibility. Applications can be made ex-parte, without the necessity of informing or involving the child's parents or any other person. In this way, it is possible to obtain the court order very quickly indeed. The order lasts for eight days only and can be extended for a further seven days. After 72 hours, an application for its discharge can be made.

The child assessment order

This order is a new concept, the above replacing orders already in existence. Although a local authority may feel that a child is at risk there are times when it cannot gain access to the child to compile evidence. In the past the local authority could apply for a place of safety order and remove the child immediately from its home. It could also do nothing. The child assessment order has effect for seven days maximum. With such an order it is possible to remove a child from its home. There is no parental responsibility. The intention behind the order is to enable the local authority to assess the child so it can make the necessary arrangements after consideration.

Before the Children's Act came into being, it was possible to make orders giving a local authority the right to intervene in a child's life under a number of jurisdictions, some overlapping. The Children's Act is now the only jurisdiction under which a local authority may act. By section 31 (4) an application for a care order or a supervision order can be made on its own or within family proceedings as defined by section 8 (3) of the Act. Applications for education supervision orders, emergency protection orders and child assessment orders have to made alone.

Categories of applicants for orders are limited to the following:

Care orders, supervision orders and child assessment orders-only a local authority or NSPCC may apply. Education supervision orders-only a local education authority may apply. Emergency protection orders-only a local authority may apply.

In place of previous powers to make different orders, the court now has intermediate powers under section 37. Where a court is dealing with family proceedings in which a question relating to the welfare of a child arises, it may direct the local authority to carry out investigations. The local authority must respond and decide what order should be applied for. If the local authority decides not to apply for an order the court cannot make it do so, although this fact must be reported to the court.

Grounds on which a court will grant an order (s 31(2))

A court has to be satisfied of the following before granting an order:
(a) that the child has suffered or is likely to suffer significant harm;
(b) that the harm or likelihood of harm is attributable to the care given to the child, or likely to be given to him if the order were not made or the child being beyond parental control.

Proof of the ground in section 31(2) only entitles accoutre to grant a care or supervision order. The court does not have to grant such an order. The grounds in this section are referred to as "threshold" grounds.

In relation to education and supervision orders, the court has to be satisfied that the child is of compulsory school age and not being properly educated.

To obtain an emergency protection order, the local authority must demonstrate the following:

(a) a local authority must show that the enquiries are being frustrated and that access to the child is required urgently;
(b) the NSPCC must show that it has reasonable cause to suspect that the child is in danger of suffering significant harm;
(c) any other applicant must show that there is reasonable cause to believe that the child is likely to suffer significant harm if he is not removed from the home.

As with the other orders, applications for emergency protection orders are subject to section 1 of the Act. For child assessment orders, the court has to be satisfied that:
(a) the applicant has reasonable cause to suspect that the child is suffering or likely to suffer significant harm;
(b) this can only be determined by an assessment of the child's health or development;

(c) it is not likely that an assessment can be made without an order.

Again, applications for this order are subject to section 1 of the children Act.

Parental contact

By section 34 of the Act a local authority is under a duty to allow reasonable contact between a child in care and his parents. If there is any dispute on the reasonableness of contact, the court can regulate. In limited circumstances, a local authority can refuse to allow contact for up to seven days.

By section 43, if a child is to be kept away from home during the currency of the child assent order, the order must contain directions for such contact between the child and other persons as the court thinks fit.

By section 44, an applicant who is granted such an order is placed under a duty to allow reasonable contact between child and parents.

Wardship

Wardship is the means by which the family court fulfils its jurisdiction of protection of children. When a child becomes a ward of court, the court controls its upbringing by a series of orders.

The Children and Young Persons Bill

As mentioned in the introduction to this book, The Children's and Young Persons Bill was introduced in the House of Lords on 14th November 2007. The purpose of the bill is to reform the statutory framework for the care system by implementing the proposals in the June 2007 white paper, Care Matters: Time for Change that require primary legislation. It includes provision in relation to private fostering, child death notification to Local Safeguarding Children's Boards and the secretary of state's powers to conduct research and applications for the discharge of emergency protection orders. The bill also amends the public law framework for safeguarding and promoting children's welfare through amendments to the services that are to be provided to support children and their families and the procedures to protect children who are at risk of suffering harm. The key legislation to be amended is The Children's Act 1989, The Children (Leaving Care) Act 2000, The Adoption and Children Act 2002 and the Children Act 2004.

In summary, the bill:

- enables local authorities to delegate their functions in relation to looked after children to providers of social work services;
- prevents local authorities from placing looked after children outside their area unless it is consistent with a child's welfare and the care provision is not available within the LA area;
- prevents local authorities from moving a looked after child from a local authority placement with a LA foster parent or a children's home, unless it was decided to do so as a consequence of a statutory review of a child's case;
- amends LA duties relating to the appointment of the Independent Reviewing Officer;
- extends the duties of local authorities to appoint an independent person to visit, befriend and advise any looked after child if it is in the child's best interests;
- places a duty on governing bodies of maintained schools to appoint a member of staff to be responsible for promoting the educational achievement of registered looked after pupils;
- extend the local authorities duties to appoint a personal advisor and keep the pathway plan under regular review for young people who are former relevant children and who start or resume a programme

of education and training after the age of 21 but under the age of 25;
- requires a local authority to pay a bursary to a former relevant child (i.e. a care leaver) who goes on to higher education;
- extends the powers of local authorities to make cash payments to children in need and their families;
- makes provision to enable registration authorities to issue compliance notices to children's home providers who are failing to meet national standards and to impose a notice to prevent new admissions to establishments where this is deemed appropriate;
- amend the procedures around reporting child deaths;

There are other amendments in the legislation, the above of which are key. The bill is in five parts:
- Part 1 clauses 1-6 deals with arrangements for the provision of social work services
- Part 2 clauses 7-28 principally amends the Children's Act 1989 Part 3 in respect of local authority duties when providing accommodation for looked after children; the power to establish a national IRO service; arrangements for local authorities representatives to visit children and young people living away from home; the appointment of independent visitors to looked after children; extends the entitlements of former looked after children; amends the CSA through the enforcement of national standards in children's homes; extends the powers of local authorities to make cash payments to children in need and their families; and removes the restrictions on courts to hear applications to discharge an emergency protection order.
- Part 3 Clauses 29-31 amends the Children's Act 1989 Sch 2 to allow for an independent review of the suitability of local authority foster parents.

- Part 4 clauses 32-34 makes amendments to the Children's Act 1989 Part 1 in relation to residence orders and special guardianship orders.
- Part 5 clauses 35-40 contains general and financial provisions.

Chapter 12

Rights of Adolescents

Over the last two decades in particular, the approach of the law in relation to the child has been centred on the development of children's rights. The courts have considered their wishes in accordance with the age and development of the child. Children's rights to self-determination are not absolute but incremental. In this regard, the law has recognised three ages of children's rights, including the rights of the unborn, the rights of infants and children and the rights of adolescents.

The foetus and rights

Whilst a foetus doesn't have rights in its own name, it is protected before birth and when born a person can sue for injuries inflicted whilst in the womb. In the case Paton v British Pregnancy Advisory Service, 1978 Sir George Baker laid out what is still the legal position:

The foetus cannot, in English law, in my view, have any rights of its own at least until it is born and has a separate existence from the mother. This permeates the whole of the civil law of this country.

The law embodies, within it, protection for the foetus and born infant. Whilst it may be the case that the foetus has no rights of its own, it has always been a matter of moral ethics and public policy to protect the foetus. The law has assured the foetus some legal status through legal protection which depends on the stage of gestational development. The more the gestational development the more the legal protection. In this regard, a foetus that is capable of being born alive is distinguished from a foetus that is not, for the purposes of criminal law. The common law's purpose in this regard has been to ensure that the unborn foetus is protected to ensure that it can be born.

In 1967, the Abortion Act legalised abortion, or the destruction of the foetus under certain prescribed conditions, including the danger of mental or physical ill-health to the mother or that the child born would be severely handicapped.

Rights of infants and young children

Parents and those with parental responsibility have the obligation and duty to protect a child in their care, as do local authorities and the court in wardship. However, the small child, unlike a foetus, can express a view and can be heard. The question of the young child's right to participate and be consulted and to speak and be heard in legal decisions which will affect it, has been dependant on the issue in question and is a right which exists proportionate to age, understanding and development of the child.

The Children's Act 1989 s 1 (3)(a) requires the court, in exercising its jurisdiction over any matters relating to the care and upbringing of the child or in relation to the child's property to consider the 'ascertainable wishes and feelings of the child concerned considered in the light of his age and understanding'. The child's voice is heard through appointing a children's guardian who speaks on behalf of the child.

The weight the court will attach to those wishes and feelings will depend upon whether the court considers the wishes and feelings to be truly those held by the child; to what extent it considers the child's expression of wishes and feelings are sentiments a child can hold and whether those wishes expressed are in the child's best interests.

One case which illustrates this is that in Re J and K (Abduction: Objections of Child) 2005, the mother had two children. One child, nearly nine years old was the son of the mothers husband. The younger child was almost five years old and the son of a man with whom the mother had cohabited. The mother's second relationship ended and she left the children in the care of her former partner, who arranged for the elder boy to live with his own father, the younger boy remaining in the care of the former partner for a few weeks, until the mother returned and could care for the younger child and at some time later care for the elder boy. The mother removed the two children from Malta, where they were living. The Children and Family Court Advisory Service reported that the nine year old did not wish to return to Malta. The court granted the fathers application for the return of the children to Malta, and held that its decision to take account of a child's stated objection to being returned to the state of habitual residence did not relieve the court the task of deciding, in the discretionary analysis, what weight to afford the objection. In this case, the child's stated objection was to returning to the care of paternal grandparents, whereas the father had provided an undertaking not to bring the child into contact with the grandparents.

The rights of the adolescent

The law gives more weight to the right of an adolescent to be heard. This is because he or she is approaching the age of 18 where, officially at least, adulthood is reached.

When it comes to the law concerning adolescent competence, there are two considerations. First, the Family Law Reform Act 1969 s8, gives a 16 to 17 year old the right to consent to their own medical treatment. However, there is no right to say no to treatment. The consent of the child can be given regardless of the views of the parents.

Secondly, what is known as the 'Gillick competence' test also applies to a child of 16-17 years old, as well as applying to a child under 16 to any matter not solely related to a medical question. The Gillick test arises from the case of Gillick v West Norfolk and Wisbech Health

Authority (1986) where the House of Lords ruled that a child's right to determine her own treatment (in this case contraceptive treatment) where she was considered competent, prevailed over and above the parental right to determine the issue on her behalf. This was a landmark case which changed the basis of thinking in this respect.

Where the child is under 16, the law has recognised that the young person is able to participate and make decisions, notwithstanding that he or she has not reached the age of 18. The law has recognised the importance of the child's views even when they conflict with those of the parents or other adults who have responsibility for them. Such children are called 'Gillick competent'.

In determining whether a child is Gillick competent, the courts have taken into account age, understanding and maturity. Although chronological age is important there is no fixed age in relation to any question and the age at which the child would be considered competent would depend on the issue in question.

Chapter 13

Making a Will

The main principle underlying any will is that, if you have possessions, own property etc then you need to organise a will which will ensure that chosen people benefit after your death.

In the majority of cases, a person's affairs are relatively uncomplicated and should not involve the use of a solicitor.

There are certain basic rules to be followed in the formation of a will and if they are then it should be legally binding.

The only inhibiting factor on the disposal of your assets will be any tax liability following death, which will be dealt with later in this book. There are a number of other factors to consider, however:

- Age of person making a will

A will made by anyone under the age of eighteen, known as a minor, will not be valid unless that person is a member of the services (armed forces) and is on active service.

- Mental health considerations

A will formed by a person, who was insane at the time of writing, will not be valid. Mental illness in itself is not a barrier to creating a will, as long as proof can be shown that the person was not insane at the time of writing.

Subsequent mental illness, following the formation of a will, will not be a barrier to a will's validity.

Definition of insanity

Insanity, or this particular condition, will normally apply to anyone certified as such and detained in a mental institution. In addition, the Mental Health Act covers those in " a state of arrested or incomplete development of mind which includes sub-normality of intelligence and is of such a nature or degree that the patient is incapable of living an independent life or guarding against serious exploitation.

In any situation where there is doubt as to a persons capabilities then it is always best to have any will validated by an expert. This applies to anyone, not just those classified as insane.

The main point of any will is that, in the final analysis, a court would have to be satisfied that the contents of the will are genuine, there has not been any attempt whatsoever to alter the contents or to influence that persons mind. The person writing the will must have fashioned its contents with no outside interference.

Unfortunately, the history of the production of people's last will and testament is littered with greedy and unscrupulous persons who wish to gain from another's demise. It is necessary to be careful!

Making a will

The main reason for making a will is to ensure that you make the choice as to who you leave your possessions, and not the state. You can also impose any specific conditions you want in your will. For example, you can impose age conditions or conditions relating to the need to perform certain duties before benefiting.

If you do not make a will then, on your death, the law of intestacy will apply to the disposal of your estate. You will have had no say and certain criteria are applied by the state, which will take responsibility. In the circumstances described above, after costs such as funeral and administration of other aspects of death, an order of preference is established, as follows:

- Your spouse, which is your husband or wife
- Any children you may have. This includes all children, whether by marriage, illegitimate or adopted.
- Parents
- Brothers and sisters
- Half brothers or sisters
- Grandparents
- Uncles and aunts
- Uncles and aunts (half blood)

It is the law of intestacy that if any of the above, in that order, die before the person who is the subject of intestacy, then their children will automatically benefit in their place.

There are conditions which will affect the above order of beneficiaries:

- If the spouse of a person is still living and there are no surviving children, parents, brothers or sisters or any of their offspring living then the spouse will benefit solely
- If the spouse is still living and there is children, the estate will be divided along the following lines:

The spouse will take all the personal items and up to £75,000 if money is involved. This will be augmented by interest on the money from the date of death. There will be a life interest in half of the residue of the estate. This means use as opposed to ownership. In the case of money it relates to interest on capital only and not the capital itself;

Children (equal shares) Half the residue of the estate plus the other half on the death of the spouse.

If the spouse is still alive, there are no children but there are other relatives, such as parents, brothers and sisters and their children the following rules apply:

The spouse will have all the personal items and up to £125000 if it is available, interest on money and half the residue of the estate;

Parents will receive half the residue or, if there are no parents alive then brothers and sisters will, in equal shares, keep half the residue.

By law, the spouse is entitled to carry on living in the matrimonial home after death. The matrimonial home is defined as the place where he or she had been living at the time of death.

If there is no spouse living but there are children then the estate will be divided equally between them. This will occur when they are over the age of eighteen or marry, whichever occurs first.

If there is no spouse and no children but there are parents, then the estate will be divided equally between them. If there is no spouse, no children and no parents, then the estate will be divided equally between brothers and sisters. If there are no brothers and sisters then half brothers and sisters. If none, grandparents. If not, uncles and aunts and if none to half blood uncles and aunts. As can be seen, the law of intestacy tries to ensure that at least someone benefits from a person possessions on death. There is a ranking order and in most cases there would be someone to benefit. There are certain categories of person who fall outside of the law of intestacy, even though there may have been some connection in the past:

Divorced Persons

There is no right of entitlement whatsoever for a divorced person to benefit from an estate on death. This right ceases from the decree absolute.

Separated persons

If a separation order is granted by a divorce court then there is no entitlement to benefit. If the separation is informal and there is separate habitation or a Magistrates court order has been granted for separation then there is normal entitlement.

Cohabitation

The law of intestacy dictates that, if you were living with someone, but not married, at the time of death, then that person has no direct claim to the estate. However, in practice this operates somewhat differently and there is a law, Provision for Family and Dependants Act 1975 under which cohabitees can claim. We will be discussing this a little later.

Although anyone has a right to have their estate distributed in accordance with the law of intestacy it is highly inadvisable. It is better at all time to ensure that you have complete control over where your money goes. It may be that you do not wish immediate family to benefit over others and that you wish to leave all your money to a particular favoured person or to an institution. This can only be achieved by personalising your will and remaining in control of what happens after your death.

The decision to make a will

It is essential that you make a will as soon as possible. If you leave it, there is a chance that you may never get round to doing it and may be reliant upon the state doing it for you. There is also the chance that you will leave a situation where people start to contest your possessions, fight amongst each other and fall out.

There are many things to consider when you decide to produce a will. As a person gets older, chances are that he or she will become wealthier. Savings grow, endowments increase, insurance policies become more valuable, property is purchased and so on. A bank balance in itself is no indicator of worth, as there are many other elements which add up to wealth. Changes in personal circumstances often justify the need to make a will.

- Ownership of property
- Children
- Marriage or remarriage
- Employment
- Illness
- Divorce and separation
- Increase in personal wealth, such as an inheritance

Ownership of property

Ownership of property usually implies a mortgage. If you are wise it will also imply life insurance to at least the value of the property. It is very prudent to make a will which specifies exactly to whom the property will be left. As we have seen, the law of intestacy provides for the decision if you do not have a will.

Children

As we have seen, under the law of intestacy, any children you have will benefit after your death. However, it is very sensible, under a will, to specify how and when they will benefit. It could be that you may let someone else make that decision later on. Whatever, you should make it very clear in your will.

Marriage or remarriage

The most important point to remember is that marriage or remarriage will automatically revoke the provisions of any former will, although this is not the case in Scotland. Therefore, when marrying you should make certain that your will is up to date and that you have altered the provisions. In short, you should amend your will, or produce a new will in order to outline clearly what you want your new partner to have.

Employment

You should be very aware that certain types of employment carry greater risks than others. This will necessitate producing a will as soon as possible as if you are in a high-risk category then you need to ensure that those nearest you are catered for.

Illness

Illness is something that none of us want but cannot avoid if it decides to strike. No matter how healthy you are you should take this into account when considering putting together a will. In addition, some people have a family history of illness and chances are that they too could suffer. Therefore illness is a very real motivator for producing a will.

Divorce and separation

The law of intestacy states that if you die your divorced spouse loses all rights to your estate. You may not want this to happen and make provisions in your will. Although children of any marriage will benefit it could be that you may wish to make slightly different provisions for different children.

Increase in personal wealth

Financial success, and inheritance will increase your wealth and inevitably make you estate more complicated. It is absolutely essential to ensure that you have a will and that you are updating that will regularly to take into account increased assets.

The provisions of a will

Having considered some of the many reasons for producing a will, it is now necessary to look at exactly what goes into a will. Essentially, the purpose of a will is to ensure that everything you have accumulated in your life is disposed of in accordance with your own desires. The main areas to consider when formulating a will are:

- Money you have saved, in whatever form
- Any buildings (property) you have
- Any land you have
- Any insurance policies you have. This is of utmost importance
- Any shares you may own
- Trusts set up
- Any other personal effects

Money you have saved

Money is treated as part of your wider estate and will automatically go to those named as the main beneficiaries. However, you might wish to make individual bequests to other people outside your family. These have to be specified. When including any provisions in your will relating to money, you should be very clear about the whereabouts of any saving accounts or endowments, premium bonds etc. Life becomes very difficult if you have left sums of money but there is no knowledge of the whereabouts of this. Inevitably, solicitors have to be employed and this becomes very expensive indeed.

Property

It is necessary to make provisions for any property you have. If you are the sole owner of a property then you can dispose of it as you wish. Any organisation with a superior interest would take an interest, particularly if there are mortgages outstanding. It is important to remember that if you are a joint owner of a property, such as a joint tenancy, then on death this joint ownership reverts to the other joint owner, bringing it into sole ownership.

Leasehold property can be different only in so much as the executor of an estate will usually need permission before assigning a lease. This can be obtained from the freeholder.

Land

Although the same principles apply to land as to property, indeed often the two are combined, in certain circumstances land may be owned separately. In this case the land and everything on it can be left in the will.

Insurance policies

The contents of any insurance policy needs to be checked carefully. In certain cases there are restrictions on who can benefit on death. Particular people may be specified and you have no alternative but to let such people benefit, even though your own circumstances may have changed. If there are no restrictions then you can bequeath any money as you see fit.

Shares

Shares can normally be bequeathed in a will as anything else. However, depending on the type of share, it is just possible that there may be restrictions. One such situation is where shares are held in a private company and there may be a buy back clause.

Trusts

Trusts can be set up for the benefit of family and friends. However, a trust, by its very nature is complex as the law dealing with trusts is complex. It is absolutely essential, if you are considering setting up a trust to get specialist advice.

Personal effects

Although you are perfectly entitled to leave specific items of personal effects in your will, such legacies are separate from those of other possessions such as money or land.

The law recognises that in some cases there may not be enough money to pay expenses related to your death. Any money owed will be retrieved from any financial gifts you have outlined. However, personal effects cannot be touched if you have clearly identified these in your will. This includes items of value such as jewellery.

It is not enough to be general on this point. You must specify exactly what it is you are leaving and to whom. Remember, certain gifts will be taxable. We will be covering this in chapter

The funeral

It is common practice to include such matters as how you wish to be buried, in what manner and the nature of the ceremony, in your will. You should discuss these arrangements with your next of kin in addition to specifying them in your will as arrangements may be made for a funeral before details of a will are made public. Another way is to detail your wishes in a letter and pass this on to your executor to ensure that the details are known beforehand. There is no reason why any of your instructions should not be carried out, subject to the law. However, your executor can override your wishes if necessary and expedient. You can, in addition, make known your wishes for maintenance of your grave after your death. Agreement of the local authority, or relevant burial authority must be sought and there is no obligation on them to do this. In addition, there is a time limit of 99 years in force.

The use of your body after death

It could be that you have decided to leave your body for medical research or donate your organs. This can be done during your final illness, in writing or in front of a minimum of two witnesses. You should contact your local hospital or General Practitioner about this, they will supply you with more details.

Making a recital

A recital consists of a statement at the end of your will which explains how and why you have drawn up a will in the way you have. This is not commonly done but sometimes may be necessary, especially if you have cut people out of your will but do not intend to cause confusion or hurt.

Recitals are sometimes necessary in order to clarify a transfer of authority to others on your death. This could be in business for example. In addition, you may wish to recognise someone's contribution to your life, for example a long serving employee or a particular friend.

Making provisions in your will

Who to name

When including persons, or organisations, in your will it is better to form a separate list right at the outset.

Naming individuals in your will

There are certain criteria which apply when naming individuals in a will, although in principle you can name who you want. Any person considered an adult, i.e. over 18, can benefit from your will. However, if a person cannot be traced within a time period of seven years after being named, or dies before you, then the amount left in your will to that person is included in what is known as the residue of your estate, what is left after all bequests. You can also make a bequest in your will to cover that eventuality, that is for another named person to benefit in his or her place.

If the bequest is to your own children or any other direct descendant and they die before you then the gift will automatically go to their children, unless there is something to the contrary in your will. In addition, if you make a gift to two or more people and one dies then that share is automatically passed to the other (joint owner).

Children

You are entitled to leave what you want in your will to children whether they are illegitimate or stepchildren. Stepchildren should be stipulated in your will. If children are under 18 then it will be probably necessary to leave property such as land, in trust for them until they reach 18 or any other age stated in the will. No child under 18 can be a trustee. Those people who are not British citizens, i.e. foreigners can benefit from your will in the same way as anyone else.

The only real restriction to this is if there is a state of war between your own country and theirs, in which case it will be necessary to wait until peace is declared.

Mental illness

There is nothing currently in law which prevents a person suffering mental illness from receiving a bequest under a will. Obviously, depending on the state of mind of that person it could be that someone may have to accept the gift and take care of it on the persons behalf.

Bankruptcy

If a person is either bankrupt or facing bankruptcy then if that person receives a gift there is a chance that it could end up in the hands of a creditor. To avoid this happening you can establish a protective trust which will enable the person in receipt of the gift to enjoy any interest arising from the gift during a specific time.

Animals

It is possible to leave money to animals for their care and well-being. There is a time limit involved for receipt of the money, which is currently a period of 21 years.

Groups

There is no problem legally with leaving money and other gifts to groups or organisations. However, it is necessary to ensure that the wording of the will is structured in a certain way. It is necessary to understand some of the legislation concerning charities, in order that your bequest can be deemed charitable.

Leaving money/gifts to charities

Many people leave bequests to charity. Major charities often give advice to individuals and other organisations on how to do that. Smaller charities can pose a problem as they may not be as sound and as well administered as larger ones. It is best to stipulate an alternative charity in the event of the smaller one ceasing to operate. If for whatever reason you bequest cannot be passed on to the group concerned then it will be left in the residue of your estate and could be liable to tax. There are a number of causes which might be deemed as charitable. These are:

- Educational causes
- Help for the community
- Animal welfare
- Help for the elderly
- Disabled

- Religious groups
- Sick, such as hospices

In the event of making a bequest to a charitable cause, it is certain that you will need expert advice, as with the setting up of trusts.

Preparing a will

One of the key rules is that there should be nothing in your will that can be ambiguous or open to interpretation. It is essential to ensure that your intentions are crystal clear. It will probably be necessary to get someone else to look at your will to ensure that it is understood by others.

Preparation of will

A will can of course be rewritten. However, it is very important indeed to ensure that you have spent enough time in the initial preparation stages of your will as it could be enacted at any time, in the event of sudden death. If your possessions are numerous then it is highly likely that the preparation stage will be fairly lengthy as the dividing up will take more thought. This gets more complicated depending on your other circumstances, such as whether you are married or single, have children, intend to leave money to organizations, etc.

You need to make a clear list of what it is you have in order to be able to achieve clarity in your will. For example, property and other possessions will take in any buildings and land you own plus money in various accounts or other forms of saving. In addition there could be jewelry and other valuables to take into account. It is necessary to quantify the current value of these possessions. It is also necessary to balance this out by making a list of any outstanding loans/mortgages or other debts you may have. Funeral costs should come into this. It is essential that you do not attempt to give away more than you actually have and also to deduce any tax liabilities from the final amount after debts. The wording of any will is always done with tax liability in mind.

Listing those who will benefit from your will

Making a list of beneficiaries is obviously necessary, including all groups, individuals and others who will benefit. With each beneficiary you should list exactly what it is that you bequeath. If a trust is necessary, then note this and note down the name of proposed trustees. These persons should be in agreement before being named. Contact any charities that will benefit. They can supply you with a legacy clause to include in your will.

The most important point, at this stage, is that you ensure that what you are leaving does not exceed the estate and that, if liable for tax, then there is sufficient left over to meet these liability.

Make a note of any recitals that you wish to include in your will and exactly what you wish to say.

The choice of an executor of your will

The job of any executor is to ensure that your will is administered in accordance with the terms therein as far as is legally possible at that time. It is absolutely essential to ask those people is they consent to being an executor. They may well refuse which could pose problems. You can ask friends or family or alternatively you can ask a solicitor or your bank. They will make a charge for this. However, they are much less likely to make a mistake in the execution of the will than an untrained individual. They will charge and this should be provided for. If you do choose to appoint an untrained executor, then it is good policy to appoint at least two in order to ensure that there is an element of double checking and that there are enough people to fulfill the required duties.

The presentation of your will

You can either prepare your will on ordinary sheets of paper or used specially prepared forms which can be obtained from stationers or book shops. Bookshops will usually sell "will packs" which take you through the whole preparation stage, from contemplation to completion.

Try to avoid handwriting your will. If it cannot be read then it will be invalid. You should always try to produce it on a word processor or typewriter. This can be more easily altered at any time.

The advantage of using a pre-printed form is that it has all of the required phrases on it and you just fill in the blanks. It just may be that you are not in the position to write your will, as you may be one of the considerable numbers of people who cannot read or write in this country. In this case, you can get someone else to write it for you although it is essential that you understand the contents. Get someone else, independent of the person who wrote it to read it back to you to ensure that the contents reflect your wishes.

The wording of a will

The wording of a will is of the utmost importance as it is absolutely necessary to ensure that you produce a clear document which is an instrument of your own will. The following are some words, which appear in wills, with an explanation of their precise meaning and pitfalls:

"beneficiary"
this means someone or something that benefits as a result of a gift in a will.

"bequeath"
"I bequeath" in a will usually refers to personal property such as personal property and money.

"children"
this includes both legitimate and illegitimate children and also adopted children. Where a gift is to a child and that child has children and dies before the death of the person making the will then the gift will pass on to the child or children of that child if they are living at the time of the testators death unless an intention to the contrary appears in the will.

"Children" does not usually include step children and if you wish a step child to be included then this will need to be specified. Children will include step children where there are only step children alive at the time of making the will.

"Children" can also include grandchildren where it is clear that this was intended or there are only grandchildren and no other children are alive at the date of making a will. You should always specify grandchildren when you want them included.

"descendants"
this means children, grandchildren, great grandchildren and so on down the line. A gift using this word is sometimes phrased "to my descendants living at my death" which includes all those who are alive at the time of the death of the person making a will. Male descendants means males who are descended from females as well as those who are descended from males. A gift to descendants means that they all take equal shares. If you wish each merely to take in default of a parent or parents (e.g. if a parent predeceases you) then add the words "per stirpes".

"devise"
"I devise" in a will usually refers to a gift of land, which includes a house.

"Executor/Executrix"
this is the person or persons you appoint to administer your will and to carry out your wishes as expressed in your will. Anyone can be appointed an executor, usually expressed as a clause in your will. The few exceptions are those of a minor and those of unsound mind. Solicitors and banks can also be appointed. Executors can also receive gifts under the will. The executor cannot charge fees, banks and solicitors do but the will must stipulate this. Because of the fact that executors can change their minds about taking on the task of administering your will, it is often better to have two.

"Family"
this word should not be used if it can be helped as it has been interpreted in several different ways. It is, by and large, far to general.

"Husband"
this means the husband at the time of making the will. In the event of a divorce, a person remains married until the decree absolute has been granted. Divorce alters the will in so far as any appointment of a former spouse as an executor becomes void, as do any bequests to that person, unless there is a contrary intention in the will. Generally, if a marriage splits up it is best to review the provisions of a will.

"Infant"
this means a child under the age of eighteen. Land is given to trustees (usually) if left to those under eighteen, as an infanr cannot hold an estate in land.

"Issue"
this means all descendants but has been interpreted as having several meanings. In a simple will its use should be avoided altogether as again, it is far too general.

"Minor"
this has the same meaning as infant.

"Nephews"
the meaning of this term depends upon the context of the will. It is far safer, in any such general situation to be specific and name names.

"Next of kin"
this means the closest blood relation.

"Nieces"
the same applies as for nephews.

"Pecuniary legacy"
this means a gift of money in a will.

"Residue"
this means the amount that is left of your estate after effect has been given to all the gifts in your will and testamentary and other expenses have been paid.

"Survivor"
this may apply to persons who are not born at the time of the will. Therefore, a gift to all those who survive a person leaving the will could include all brothers and sisters not yet born.

"Testamentary expenses"
in a will the residue of an estate may be left to a person after all expenses. This includes all known expenses, such as the costs of administering the will.

"Trustee"
a trustee is someone entrusted to look after property for another until a certain age is attained or condition fulfilled. There should always be more than one trustee with two being a usual number.

"Wife"
this means the wife at the time of making the will. Again, in the event of a divorce, then the decree absolute must be granted before that person ceases to be a wife.

Safekeeping of a will

A will must always be kept safe and should be able to be located at the time of your death. You may spend a great deal of time on your will. However, if it cannot be found then it will be assumed that you have not made one.

Any will or codicil may be deposited at Somerset House for a fee. They will send you an envelope in which to deposit your will. Seal it and complete the information on the outside, giving your name and the details of your executors. Then sign the outside of the sealed envelope in the presence of a witness or probate officer. Keep a copy of your will in case you want to refer to its contents and then either send in the sealed envelope with a covering letter to Somerset House or hand it in to any probate registry or sub registry. You will be given an official certificate that the will has been deposited and it is important that you tell your executors this.

Wills and the courts

Courts have wide powers to make alterations to a persons will, after that persons death. It can exercise these powers if the will fails to achieve the intentions of the person who wrote it, as a result of a clerical error or a failure to understand the instructions of the person producing the will.

In addition, if mental illness can be demonstrated at the time of producing the will then this can also lead to the courts intervening.

In order to get the courts to exercise their powers, an application must be made within six months of the date on which probate is taken out. If gifts or other are distributed and a court order is made to rectify the will then all must be returned to be distributed in accordance with the court order.

If any part of a persons will appears to have no meaning or is ambiguous then the court will look at any surrounding evidence and the testators intention and will rectify the will in the light of this evidence.

The right to dispose of property

In general, the law allows an unfettered right to dispose of a persons property as they choose. This however is subject to tax and the courts powers to intervene.

The law has been consolidated in the Inheritance (Provision for Family and Dependants Act) 1975. Certain categories of people can now apply to the court and be given money out of a deceased person's will. This can be done whether there is a will or not.

The husband or wife of a deceased person can be given any amount of money as the court thinks reasonable. The 1975 Act implemented the recommendations of the Law Commission which felt that a surviving spouse should be given money out of an estate on the same principles as a spouse is given money when there is a divorce. This means that, even if a will is not made, or there are inadequate provisions then a surviving spouse can make an application to rectify the situation.

The situation is different for other relations. They can apply to the court to have a will rectified but will receive far less than the spouse. The following can claim against a will:

- The wife or husband of the deceased
- A former wife or former husband of the deceased who has not remarried
- A child of the deceased
- Any person who is not included as a child of the deceased but who was treated by the deceased as a child of the family in relation to any marriage during his lifetime
- Any other person who was being maintained, even if only partly maintained, by the deceased just before his or her death

Former spouse

There is one main condition under which a former spouse can claim and that is that they have not remarried. In addition, such a claim would be for only essential maintenance which would stop on remarriage. There is one key exception, that is that if your death occurs within a year of divorce or legal separation, your former spouse can make a claim.

Child of the deceased

As the above, any claim by children can only be on the basis of hardship.

Stepchildren

This includes anyone treated as your own child and supported by you, including illegitimate children or those conceived before, but not born till after, your death. The claim can only cover essential maintenance.

Dependants

This covers a wide range of potential claimants. Maintenance only is payable. There needs to be evidence of full or partial maintenance prior to death. Such support does not have to be financial, however.

There is another situation where the court can change a will after your death. This relates directly to conditions that you may have imposed on a beneficiary in order to receive a gift which are unreasonable. If the court decides that this is the case, that particular condition becomes void and does not have to be fulfilled.

If the condition involved something being done before the beneficiary receives the gift then the beneficiary does not receive the gift. If the condition involved something being done after the beneficiary received the gift then the beneficiary can have the gift without condition.

If the beneficiary does not receive the gift, as in the above, then either the will can make alternative provision or the gift can form part of the residue of the estate. Unreasonable conditions can be many, one such being any condition that provides reason or incentive to break up a marriage, intention to remain celibate or not to remarry or one that separates children. There are others which impinge on religion, general behaviour and crime. An unreasonable condition very much depends on the perception of the beneficiary and the perception of the courts. A beneficiary can lose the right to a bequest, apart from any failure to meet conditions attached to a bequest. Again, a court will decide in what circumstance this is appropriate. Crime could be a reason, such as murder, or evidence of coercion or harassment of another person in pursuit of selfish gain.

Probate

Probate simply means that the executor's powers to administer the estate of a dead person have been officially confirmed. A document called a "Grant of Representation" is given which enables those administering the estate to gain access to all relevant information, financial or otherwise concerning the person's estate.

Although anyone charged under a will to act on behalf of the dead persons estate has automatic authority to represent, there are certain cases where evidence of probate is required. If no will exists or no executors have been appointed, then it will be necessary to obtain "letters of administration" which involves a similar procedure.

Under common law, probate has a number of objectives. These are:

- To safeguard creditors of the deceased
- To ensure reasonable provision is made for the deceased's dependants
- To distribute the balance of the estate in accordance with the intentions of the person whose will it is.

One of the key factors affecting the need to obtain probate is how much money is involved under the terms of a will. Where the sums involved are relatively small then financial institutions and other organisations will not normally want to see evidence of probate. However, it should be remembered that no on is obliged to release anything relating to a dead persons estate unless letters of administration or documents of probate can be shown. Those responsible for administering the estate must find out from the organisations concerned what the necessary procedure is.

Applying for probate

Where a will is in existence and executors have been appointed then any one of the named people can make the application. Where a will is in existence but no executors have been appointed, then the person who benefits from the whole estate should make the application. This would be the case where any known executor cannot or will not apply for probate.

Where there is no will in existence then the next of kin can apply for probate. There is an order of priority relating to the application:

- The surviving spouse
- A child of the deceased
- A parent of the deceased
- A brother or sister of the deceased
- Another relative of the deceased

The person applying for probate must be over eighteen. 'Children' includes any that are illegitimate. If a child dies before the deceased then one of his or her children can apply for probate.

Application for probate

This can be done through any probate registry or office. There is usually one in every main town and any office in any area will accept the application. If you are writing then you should always address your correspondence to a registry and not an office. You can also contact the Probate Personal Application Department at Somerset House in London, address as follows:

Probate Personal Application Department
2nd Floor
Somerset House
Strand
London
WC2R ILP
Tel: 0171 936 6983

What needs to be done next

The next of kin should register the death with the register of Births and Deaths. A death certificate will be supplied and copies of the death certificate which will need to be included to various institutions and organisations.

A copy of the will has to be obtained. The whereabouts should be known to the executors. The executor should then take a copy of the will in case the original is lost. The executor will need to obtain full details of the dead persons estate, including all property and other items together with a current valuation. It is possible that on many of the less substantial items a personal valuation can be made. It should however, be as accurate as possible.

In the case of any bank accounts a letter should be sent by the executor to the bank manager, stating that he is the executor and giving full details of the death. Details should be requested concerning the amount of money in the dead persons account(s) together with any other details of valuables lodged with the bank. The bank manager may be able to pass on information concerning holdings in stocks and shares. If share certificates are held then a valuation of the shares at time of death should be requested.

In the case of insurance policies, the same procedure should be followed. A letter should be sent to the insurance company requesting details of policies and amounts owed or payable.

In the case of National Savings Certificates the executor should write to the Savings Certificate Office in Durham and ask for a list of all certificates held, date of issue and current value. In the case of Premium Bonds a letter should be sent to the Bond and Stock Office in Lancashire Giving name and date of death. Premium Bonds remain in the draw for 12 months after death, so they can be left invested for that time or cashed in when probate has been obtained. Form SB4 (obtained from any post office) is used to inform of death and obtain repayment of most government bonds.

In the case of property, whatever valuation is put on a property the Inland revenue can always insist on its own valuation. If there is a mortgage, the executor should write to the mortgagee asking for the amount outstanding at the time of death.

The above procedure should be followed when writing to any one or an organisation, such as a pension fund, requesting details of monies owed to the dead person.

Debts owed by the person

The executor will need to compile a list of debts owed by the dead person as these will need to be paid out of the estate. These debts will include all money owed, loans, overdrafts, bills and other liabilities. If there is any doubt about the extent of the debts then the executor can advertise in the London Gazette and any newspaper which circulates in the area where the estate is situated. Efforts also have to be made to locate creditors outside of advertising. The advert will tell creditors that they have to claim by a certain date after which the estate will be administered having obtained probate.

Funeral expenses should be quantified and a letter should be sent to the Inland Revenue to determine the income tax position of the dead person.

Finally

The executor obtains the application form, decides where he or she wishes to be interviewed, send the completed form together with the death certificate and the original will to the Probate Registry and then attends for an interview.

The forms
The forms consist of the following:

- Form PR83-Probate Application form

- CAP 44-Return of the whole estate

- CAP 37 and 40-Inland Revenue Capital Taxes Office

Index

Adoption, 7, 10, 11, 15, 20, 31, 59, 63, 69, 70, 72, 73, 78, 80, 81, 82, 83, 84, 101
Adoption and Children Act 2002, 10, 20, 31, 59, 71, 72, 78, 101
Adoption of children from overseas, 10, 80
Adoptive parents, 10, 73
Alternatives to adoption orders, 11, 84
Applying for probate, 13, 131
Associated persons, 9, 62
Awards of property, 8, 39
Biological parents, 10, 69
Care orders, 12, 96, 98
Care plans, 10, 80
Child assessment order, 96
Child Support Act 1991, 52
Child Support, Pensions and Social Security Act 2000, 53, 72
Church of England wedding, 22
Civil partnership, 27, 29
Civil Partnership Act 2004, 18, 27, 73
Cohabitation, 12, 112
Committee on the Rights of the Child, 86
Contact Order, 93

Contested petitions, 8, 35
County Courts Act 1984, 60
Declaration of the Rights of the Child, 86
Definition of a parent, 10, 69
Definition of child, 86
Definition of insanity, 109
Detained people, 7, 31
Determining the father, 9, 53
Dissolution of a civil partnership, 7, 32
Divorce, 7, 21, 35, 36, 113, 114, 125
Domestic violence, 59
Domestic Violence, Crime and Victims Act 2004, 10, 68
Education supervision order, 96
Emergency protection order, 96
Establishing a trust, 8, 47
Family Law Act 1996, 62
Financial awards, 8, 39, 44, 46
Foster parents, 74
Freestanding human rights applications in family cases, 11, 89
Gender Recognition Act 2004, 18, 22
Grant of Representation, 131
Housebound people, 7, 30

Human Fertilisation and Embryology Act (HFEA) 1990, 74
Human Fertilisation and Embryology Act 1990, 53, 69
Human rights and genetic identity, 11, 84
Inherent Jurisdiction, 60
Inheritance (Provision for Family and Dependants Act) 1975, 128
Judicial Separation, 26
Law of Property Act 1925, 50
Leaving money/gifts to charities, 120
Legal parent, 71
Local Authorities failure to protect children, 90
Lump sum, 8, 41
Maintenance assessments and special cases, 9, 54
Maintenance requirement, 9, 53
Making a recital, 13, 118
Making a will, 12, 108, 109
Marriage (Prohibited Degrees of Relationship) Act 1986, 21, 23
Matching parents and children, 11, 82

Matrimonial and Family Proceeding Act 1984, 56
Matrimonial Causes Act 1973, 8, 9, 23, 36, 40, 46, 56, 66
Meaning of parental responsibility, 10, 75
Naming individuals in your will, 118
Non-Molestation Orders, 63
Nullity, 7, 22, 33
Occupation of the home, 9, 50
Occupation orders, 9, 63
Orders for the benefit of children, 8, 44
Parental contact, 12, 100
Parental responsibility, 7, 10, 31, 71, 76
Parents Rights and obligations, 69
Periodic payments, 8, 41
Placement order, 11, 83
Polygamous marriage, 25
Preparing a will, 13, 121
Probate, 13, 130, 132, 134, 135
Prohibited Steps Order, 93
Property and financial arrangements, 8, 33
Proprietary Estoppel, 50
Proving parentage, 10, 72
Psychological parents, 10, 70

Quantification of beneficial interests under a trust, 9, 49
Relevant child, 62
Residence Order, 93
Residency requirements for a civil partnerships, 29
Right to consent to medical treatment, 10, 76
Right to withhold consent for marriage, 10, 77
Rights of infants and young children, 12, 105
Rights to discipline children, 76
Safekeeping of a will, 127
Separation, 8, 32, 33
Settlement of property order, 8, 41
Specific Issues Order, 93, 94
Step-parents, 10, 73, 79
Supervision orders, 12, 96, 97
The balance of harm test, 9, 64
The Child Support Agency, 9, 52
The Children Act 1989, 9, 57
The Children and Young Persons Bill, 100
The decision to make a will, 12, 112
The definition of marriage, 7, 21
The divorce process, 8, 35

The Domestic Proceedings and Magistrates Court Act 1978, 44
The European Convention on Human Rights, 11, 89
The Family Law Act 1996, 8, 9, 39, 59, 61
The foetus and rights, 12, 104
The formalities of marriage, 7, 21
The Gender Recognition Act 2004, 21
The Gillick test, 106
The Ground For Divorce, 36
The Marriage Act 1949, 21, 23
The Protection from Harassment Act 1997, 9, 67
The provisions of a will, 13, 115
The registration of a civil partnership, 28
The rights of the adolescent, 12, 106
The use of your body after death, 118
Transfer of property, 8, 41
Trusts, 13, 47, 115, 116
Unmarried Partners, 46
Unreasonable behaviour, 32
Variation of settlement order, 41
Void marriages, 23

voidable marriages, 22
Wardship, 12, 14, 76, 100

Wills and the courts, 127